Can My Child Play?

The Questions We Should Have Asked

Marty McNair

CAN MY CHILD PLAY?
The Questions We Should Have Asked

Copyright © 2020 Martin Mcnair

First paperback edition June 2020

Developmental Editing by Lisa McAuliffe
Foreword by Ellis McKennie

ISBN: 978-1-7348177-0-6
ISBN: 978-1-7348177-2-0 (ebook)

Published by Martin McNair
https://thejordanmcnairfoundation.org/

To my son,
Jordan Martin McNair

CONTENTS

Foreword

My name is Ellis McKennie. I grew up with Jordan McNair. I played little league baseball with him, was on his high school team at McDonogh and we played football together at the University of Maryland. It always felt like Jordan and I were connected through our shared experiences. After Jordan passed, this connection became stronger than I could have imagined.

Jordan is gone, but he will always be a part of our lives. In fact, there are moments when I feel like he is still with us. I am not much for superstitions, but since Jordan's death I can't help but notice the signs in front of me. In fact, our teammate, Brendan Moore, pointed out a few events too coincidental to ignore.

Jordan's funeral was a beautiful, sunny day, right until his casket was lowered into the ground. At that moment, the skies opened, and a torrential downpour began.

Our first game without Jordan was at FedEx Field against the Texas Longhorns. It was the same matchup as our opener the year before, when Jordan got his first college minutes.

During the first offensive snap of the game, we lined up in a missing-man formation in honor of the void we all felt without Jordan that day. We were winning until the 3rd quarter when Texas went on a 22-0 run. At the beginning of the 4th quarter, we regained the lead and then suddenly, it started to rain. In fact, it poured so badly, we had to take an hour-long rain delay.

We came back on the field, pulled off an upset and knew that during this game honoring Jordan, he was there.

On March 3rd, 2019, I stood in the middle of a wet thunderstorm with six of Jordan's teammates as we wished our fallen friend a happy birthday.

On June 13th, 2019, on the one-year anniversary of Jordan's death, our team came together at the Cole Field House for an honorary workout. We all wore number 79 in Jordan' honor, while thunder and rain pounded against the roof outside.

When the Maryland Athletic Department held a ceremony, planting a tree in Jordan's memory, I am sure you can guess what the weather was like that morning.

Looking to rain as a sign from Jordan may be a stretch for some, or just seem like a way for his friends to feel closer to him. But I believe it is a constant reminder of the impact he made on our lives. I can only hope this book will make a similar impact for others.

Since the events of this book, Jordan's father Marty has dedicated his life to building a legacy for his son. Marty recognized the bigger issue surrounding Jordan's death and is determined to prevent it from happening again.

Marty has been a second father to me and several other young men who were affected by Jordan's death. When so many of us were beating ourselves up over what we could have done, Marty was a beacon of hope and light, showing us how a real man faces adversity. Instead of hanging his head down and mourning, Marty turned his pain into purpose, creating The Jordan McNair Foundation and now writing this book.

Marty's book is warning, but it also tells an important story, Jordan's story. I hope it provides you with crucial information, but more importantly, I hope it helps you get to know my friend and to understand how devastating it was to lose him.

I was honored when Marty asked for me to prepare a foreword for *Can My Child Play?* I am excited to see the impact it has on youth sports. I am even more excited for it to spread Jordan's story so that his legacy can continue forever.

Ellis McKennie

Teammate, Friend, Brother to #79

P.S. If you are currently reading this and it is raining outside, know that you are not alone.

PART I

Be Better Than Me

There is nothing quite like the feeling of having a child—of knowing you created a life. Paternal love for a child is indescribable. You instantly take on a role of protector, provider and developer all at once.

You discover you can shape this little person like a piece of clay into your vision of a successful human being. You can mold a doctor, a golfer, an astronaut, a lawyer, or any vision of success you may have. You have the ability to give them every single thing imaginable for their success. Here is your own little person that can be a mini version of your current self or the mini version of your best self you always wanted to be.

From the moment my son Jordan Martin McNair was born, I knew I wanted to mold him into a better version of myself. I embraced fatherhood head on, because I was confident that with Jordan, I had an opportunity in front of me.

An opportunity to give my son the tools he needed to be better than I was.

And when he suddenly passed away at the age of 19, he was.

Jordan was everything I could have ever imagined a son to be. Even in his death, Jordan was able to make an impact not only on his friends and family, but on the world of sports as well. It wasn't the type of impact I thought he would make all of those years ago when he was born—but it is an impact that I know will help the world be a better place. This is something I could have never purposefully molded my child into, no matter how hard I tried.

Jordan was a great kid. Not just in the way that every parent thinks their child is great. He was caring and kind. He was a Division 1 football player at the University of Maryland, but still called home for permission to go out with his friends. He had a wide, gap-toothed smile that was proportionate to his 6'5" 300-pound frame, yet almost so absurdly large that you couldn't help but smile back at it. And he had an energy that lightened your mood every time you talked to him.

By the time I was 19, I was already a statistic on the West Side of Baltimore City. My poor decision making started at an early age and by that time, my need to fit in with the wrong crowd was leading me toward nothing but drug use and jail time.

Growing up, I didn't know much about what it took to be a father. In fact, I only remember three fathers in my community. There was my next-door neighbor, Mr. Green, Mr. Billy, who used to take me to basketball games and Mr. Bagwell, my 13 Under Baltimore Neighborhood Basketball League coach. My dad was not one of those present fathers.

I only spent time with my father in summer, when my mom would send me to Denver to see him. My father was in the Air Force. While we laugh about it now, he didn't have a clue about how to raise a son. Even when I would visit in the summer, his bachelor lifestyle took precedence over developing his child.

I remember two things my father taught me during those summers. One, was how to tell time. The other was to always keep 30 days' worth of clean underwear. When I had Jordan, I wanted to pass on more than a few pieces of practical knowledge.

But it wasn't until I became a father myself that I realized just how much I had learned from my own dad. There were lessons in all of the things he *didn't* do. Mistakes he made. And they were mistakes I was determined not to repeat with Jordan.

My father left for the military at a young age and had limited interaction with his own father. He did the best that he could with the information that he had. I'm sure if he and my mother hadn't separated while I was so young, he'd have the time and opportunity to help mold me into something more. It is impossible to successfully raise a child from halfway across the country. The distance between us made it nearly inconceivable for him to truly know what was happening in my life.

My father had no idea of the obstacles I was facing, or of the trauma I had experienced. He had no idea that a babysitter molested his son when he was just five years old. I never knew how that experience would negatively impact my life in the way that it did and how it would haunt me for so long. My father didn't know either. He never asked. In fact, no one ever asked about it. It was something I buried down deep inside. Something I thought was hidden. But it was a pain that would follow me for years and manifest in ways that would seriously impact the trajectory of my life.

By the time I was 13, I had already started making poor life decisions. At 13, my son Jordan decided to put his energy into football. When I was selling my first nickel bag of marijuana, Jordan got accepted to the McDonough School as a rising freshman. My freshman year, I got arrested and kicked out of school for smoking a joint at lunch. When Jordan was a freshman, he was getting his first look from colleges.

At a time in Jordan's life when he was building a real future for himself, I was on my way to becoming a statistic; another stereotype of a young black male in Baltimore City who was nothing but trouble. I had been arrested and was on probation at the time. More importantly, I had gone through a "rite of passage" in a social circle that valued street cred over everything else.

Where I grew up, the idea of social acceptance was so distorted, it all came down to three things. One, how good you could fight. Two, if you could get arrested and prove you wouldn't snitch on your friends. And three, if you went to jail and you weren't afraid to stand up, fight for yourself and not let anyone take advantage of you. Then you would come home with a sense of street cred. That's what it took to fit in, and it is still the same way for so many young men in inner-city communities today.

In these microcosms of American culture, there is a need for social acceptance. The need to prove you belong. And violence is the only currency that people acknowledge and respect. In the movie *Goodfellas*, when Henry Hill's character gets arrested for the first time, he is released to his older mob friends. They celebrate his first arrest like it was his high school graduation—the first meaningful accomplishment in his life. He took his first arrest like a man. He didn't say anything and most importantly, he didn't tell on his friends. This was the acceptance that I wanted, and that we all wanted, growing up.

Don't get me wrong, my mother was successful. We lived in a beautiful upper middle-class neighborhood, where the majority of my friends didn't live. My mother loved and supported me unconditionally. When I got in trouble, she picked me up in the middle of the night from the police station, even though she had work in the morning. When I got kicked out of school, she made sure I got all of my school assignments from my teachers and returned them completed. She paid for my first lawyer with the money that could have purchased my first car.

In fact, my first lawyer as a juvenile delinquent, is our current legal team's journeyman. The prominent civil rights attorney and former judge William H. "Billy" Murphy Jr. was so vested in my success that he agreed to give my mother half of her money back if I passed to the next grade in school.

When our paths crossed again under these unfortunate series of events, I reminded him of our first meeting. I remember him asking me if I knew what "in by five, married by six" meant. He let me know back then that prison was a brutal place, that only the strong survived and the weak were preyed upon. I was going in a direction I thought I wanted to go in, but back then, I couldn't see that I could do better.

William Murphy had me tell that story quite a few times when we met back up. Everyone wanted to see me win, except for me. My mother did her best to keep me out of trouble. She wanted to push me to do better, to *be better.* However, the allure of Baltimore's fast life had a stronger pull on me than my own mother did.

At an age when my son Jordan was preparing for his 16th birthday party, my bad decisions were only gaining momentum. By 16, my cries for help were getting louder. My trauma expressed itself in bad decision after bad decision. I was hanging with the wrong crowd, experimenting with drugs, having sex and doing everything you can imagine a 16-year-old shouldn't be doing.

I wasn't all bad though. I always had a part-time job. I was a good student when I was actually in school. I loved basketball and would play in every intramural league I could. I didn't have the discipline to play in school, though. Not like Jordan did. My fast lifestyle choices had taken precedence over that. I'd rather go to work and stand on the corner with the rest of my friends, then take on the responsibility of a team sport.

Each year on Jordan's birthday, I would always tell him where I was and what I was doing with my life at his age. And I would tell him how he could be better than I was. I would always tell him to enjoy being young. "There's no need to rush your life son. Everything you need to experience you will when the time is right." I never wanted him to live fast the way that I did. I wanted him to learn from my experiences. I wanted his life to be better than mine.

When Jordan was 18 years old, he was on his way to the University of Maryland to play football. At 18, I was on my way to Cheyney University in Pennsylvania as a first-generation college student.

The only difference in our stories was that Jordan's mother and I had co-parented and developed a young man who would be successful with our support no matter what. We made a choice to make Jordan's development a priority. My mother did the best she could supporting me, but she also made her own bad decisions. And her choice to love a mentally abusive partner, paired with a rebellious teenage son, took its toll on her over time.

7

No one told me what I was supposed to do in college, besides just going through the motions of being a student. When Jordan got to college, I encouraged him to join a Greek fraternity to create a lifelong brotherhood of relationships that he could benefit from. At his age, I didn't have the foresight or support to want to be a part of something beyond what I was doing at that moment.

So, I did what I usually did, I hung out with the cool crowd. I was getting a degree from Streets and Corners University, instead of focusing on the educational opportunity in front of me. It had more value to me at that time than getting a real degree from Cheyney. It didn't matter that I made it to college, or that I was attending one of the first historically black universities in the country. Even in college, the allure of the streets and the fast life rang louder in my ears than getting an education.

While I was at school, my so-called friends were at home receiving lengthy prison sentences. Some were becoming dealers; others were becoming murder victims. Even though I had physically made it out of that environment, I couldn't let go of it mentally. Despite all of this, my mother had more tolerance and patience with me than anyone could imagine. When they say a mother's love is truly unwavering for her children—I suppose this is what they mean. Yet, no matter how much my mother loved me, every opportunity I had to go back to Baltimore, I took.

It was a time in my life where I was pushing every boundary, despite what I had in front of me. At 19, Jordan was making his entire family proud. He made the University of Maryland football team. He had friends. He was studying hard. He was thriving in college. While I was proud to have a D1 student athlete, I was most proud of Jordan's everyday accomplishments. That he was more interested in playing video games with the kids down the hall than going out to party. That he could get his groceries on his own without his mom around. That he was happy in the moment and enjoying all of the little things that make college such a formative time in your life.

I was elated that literally all of his experiences were better than mine at that age. At this age, I was almost every statistic but dead. I'd been arrested, used drugs, was on probation and I was on the fast track to throwing my entire life away. Here was my only son, Jordan, a young black man from Baltimore that wasn't a predictable statistic by 19.

I spent my son's entire life determined to make him better than me. And at 19, Jordan was already so much better of a person than I was, when this wonderful, promising life of his was cut short.

A Better Me

It was always one of my main goals as a father to raise Jordan to be better than me. I am confident it is the goal of most parents. A mother's love for her child is instinctive and protective in its own way; and while sometimes more subtle, a father's love is as equally significant. It is difficult to be a provider, protector, teacher and disciplinarian. But most of all, it is hard to be a good example of a man first and a father second. It's a unique challenge to be able to actually show your children what *to do* instead of what not to do.

A lot of times our parenting playbooks come from our own parent's techniques. Then we add our life experiences on top of that, what we think worked, what actually worked, what we learned—and we use it all to try to better our children.

I had more information and experiences that didn't work for me than I knew what to do with. So, I felt confident for 19 years that I was in the running for Father of The Year

Trophy. I had more trick plays and life lessons from all the mistakes I made than any other dad out there did. Jordan knew this, I chose never to hide this from my son.

I was 30 years old by the time I had Jordan and had a big enough playbook of past mistakes to help make sure my son was set up for success. I like to say that my life between the ages of 19 to 25 was consumed as a new wave sharecropper. I, like so many, kept the wheels of addiction, police and judicial systems spinning.

My drug use consistently caused me to make poor decision after poor decision, which led to more arrests. My mother's hard-earned bail money, taxpayer money, all used to take care of me while I was in jail. It was always for idiotic offenses, things I truly should have been able to avoid. For 30 days, 60 days, 90 days, I would sit in jail. I would convince myself I would never use again. Then I'd be back. Just keeping the wheel spinning, spinning, spinning.

I played my part as the stereotypical heroin addict. The one whose bad decisions elude reason. But man, was I keeping the system working. Officer Jones who arrested me for picking cotton, Correctional Officer Brown who serviced me pre-trial, Judge Green who sentenced me and Correctional Officer Smith who took care of me in prison—I was keeping them all working. Of course, there was still my Probation and Parole Officer Thomas and the substance abuse programs I'd try when I got out—I kept playing my part and the systematic wheel kept spinning.

I never used in jail. This decision usually came after the white-knuckle experience of heroin withdrawal. From the moment I got there, I knew what was to come. I had been through it so many times, it was rather **methodical**. I would lie on the cold, dirty floors of a bullpen with 20 other addicts, all going through withdrawal, all knowing what we were about to endure. There was the 5-7 days of insomnia. The diarrhea, cold sweats, hot flashes, body aches. And then there was the wishful hope for death—thinking that anything would be better than experiencing this.

The sad part about it was that the anxiety of withdrawal was always the mental trigger that started the process. Once that arresting officer put those handcuffs on you, it would start because you knew what was to follow. I'd been through it enough times unfortunately to know the phrase "junk in, junk out" all too well. That experience was usually a deterrent to continue using while incarcerated even if it was just for a short period of time.

Jail becomes a respite of sorts, some people continue to use while incarcerated, which creates another set of problems, but for some people it's a chance to get clean. I never used while doing those 30 to 60-day stays. I guess you can say it was one of the few good decisions I made during that time.

I never wanted to use again when I got released. However, I had no solid information on how to stay clean. So, I would make the choice to return to the same environment and to be around the same people. It would always eventually produce the same results, every time. That animalistic existence is never far from the front of my mind, even with 25 years of sobriety behind me.

The train of long-term incarceration was en route to pick me up. It was getting closer and closer to my platform. In those days, people I knew who got clean usually got clean in prison. The respite of getting yourself together mentally and physically works in some people's favor. I knew that if I could get a long enough reprieve from my drug use, I could break the habit. Then, one day, that break came.

I was sentenced to 18 months in prison—and I knew I'd emerge a better person than I was when I went in. I just needed to be motivated to make the change.

The Silver Lining

Getting sentenced to a lengthy prison stay ended up being one of the best things that would happen to me—even if I didn't know it in the moment. I was always looking for the silver lining whenever I was incarcerated. While getting clean was always an added benefit, it didn't make these stints seem any shorter or any more bearable. You grab ahold of whatever goodness you can when you're locked up, just so you can make it through.

Fortunately, for me, there was some goodness. There was Tonya.

Tonya and I met when I was in my early twenties through our mutual friend, Karen. Tonya's love has always been unwavering, even during times when I didn't know how to love myself. She has been my rock since I met her—and most importantly, she is the reason I had my most precious gift, my son Jordan.

Tonya provided unwavering love and support at a time when I was trying to figure life out. The discussions we would have in those visiting rooms helped develop me into the man and father I have become. Although her choices weren't mine, her choice to support me during this time in my life was beneficial to us both and to the foundation we would build together.

Luckily, I was always close enough to Baltimore that she could visit me when I was locked up. Even though it was probably quite hard for her and even though it was *my* string of bad decisions that got me there in the first place, she still came. I think I would have thrown in the towel on myself back in those days, but I'm eternally grateful that she didn't.

We never could have known back then where our journey would eventually go. That years later we would have this beautiful child together. That we would separate shortly after. That we would grow even closer in our roles as co-parents. And that when this beautiful, little boy was 19, he would be taken from us.

Tonya and I have been a part of each other's stories for so long, we even started to look alike. In fact, when the media began surrounding us following Jordan's accident, most people assumed we were together, simply because of our chemistry.

I'm a firm believer that the universe makes no mistakes and that everything happens as it should. While we didn't work together as couple, I know that she was put in my life to help make me a better person—the person that I am today.

Today, with decades of sobriety behind me, I am fortunate enough to do a lot of traveling out of Baltimore Washington International Airport. Every single time I walk through the crowded, echoing terminal, I think about my last arrest. The one that changed everything. And how it happened for a reason—to help get me out of my self-destructive cycle and on to a new, better phase of my life.

It was February 7th, 1995. My clean date. I just got a job at the airport, I don't remember what I was doing exactly, some type of food delivery. I was always told it is better to have a job when you go to court for sentencing. Usually, judges are a little more lenient when you have a job—and man, did I want leniency. I had already been hired and the last thing I had to do was go get a national security check to see if there were any open warrants for my arrest.

I went in for the check and was escorted to a back office. It is not supposed to take long, you just have to sit there and wait for the free and clear signal. I was feeling pretty much as good as I could about my current situation, just sitting and waiting. Sitting and waiting.

And then, an airport police officer came through the office door. He gives me a look, briefly goes to the counter and then approaches.

"Are you Martin McNair?"

"Yes."

"I have a warrant for your arrest."

The officer walked me out of the office and into the hallway. Two plain clothes officers were waiting to escort me through another door to a holding cell under the airport. It would be two years before I would reenter society again.

My original sentence was 18 months. Now, I had additional charges and a one-year suspended sentence from a previous arrest.

With a suspended sentence, you have an option to not go to jail at the time of sentencing. You will, however, be sentenced to a probation officer you have to report to. Most importantly, you have to *not get arrested again* for that period of time. If you do get arrested for anything during that probationary period, you violated the order and you have to serve the entire suspended sentence.

I, of course, took the option that meant not going to jail. I agreed to the suspended sentence, only to get arrested a short time later. The judicial system has a way of allowing a person to hang themselves with plea bargains and suspended sentences. They are all just a way for offenders to go out and reoffend. The worst part is, for most of us, it is for an even more heinous crime than before. I am a firm advocate that jail doesn't equal treatment. However, I do believe there is an important public safety aspect to be considered. Incarcerate that addict until you can get them into a treatment program.

After being sentenced, I was sent to the Maryland Reception Diagnostic Classification Center, or the MRDCC. Here, you get evaluated on a point system. It is a list that includes your criminal history, type of crime, prior sentences and the amount of time you've been sentenced to. In my case, all the numbers added up.

The Maryland Reception Diagnostic Classification Center is a maximum-security facility where you may come out of cell a few hours a day to shower and make a phone call and not much else. Most family members know where you are by then and deep down are probably glad that you're somewhere where you can't be a drain on their daily lives.

On March 20, 1995, I turned 25 inside of this holding cell. My 25th birthday in a prison cell—what a gift for myself. It was sad but I knew I had gotten myself here. I knew I wanted to get clean, I just wasn't sure how I was going to do it.

When you're in the MRDCC, you wait and you wait for two things: the mail and the roll-out list. The roll out list tells you when you've been assigned to the institution you will start your sentence at. The average prisoner wants to get on with his or her sentence to get some normalcy and routine. A workout schedule, a religious foundation, a job, some self-help classes, getting your GED, or learning a trade—just something constructive to make the time go by.

One day, while waiting for my name on the roll-out list, I received a letter from a high school friend, Mike, who was serving an eight-year sentence at another prison. Mike had been in for a while longer than me and in his letter, he talked about *recovery,* about change, about the fact that we couldn't go back uptown thinking we could get high again.

19

I knew then that I had to make a choice. Either I was going to stop using drugs and finally live or follow the same cycle I had been for so many years—and die. Right then, I made my mind up to live from that point on.

After about 30 days in the MRDCC, my name was finally called for the roll out list. "Martin McNair, pack up you're going over to the Pen." I was momentarily elated to be leaving this place and to finally be able to start my sentence.

However, when it registered where I was going, my stomach bubbled with anxiety. This must be a mistake, the Maryland Pen, the "in by five, married by six," my lawyer once asked me about, was not where I was expecting to go.

Also known as Castle Gray Skull, the Maryland Penitentiary is the oldest, most dangerous prison in the state. Every bad prison story you can think of—takes place here. This had to be a mistake, this was my first real prison sentence.

I quickly discovered that all of the "lifers" were being moved to a new facility and Castle Gray Skull was transitioning to a low security prison for people with five years or less. However, the thought of going to this prison and all of the stigma behind it shook me to the core in a way I never expected it to and it led to an epiphany that would change my life forever.

My Epiphany

No matter how old you get, or how many life experiences you've gone through, there are always certain moments that never leave you. Ones that are so clear, you swear they could have happened just a moment ago, even when over 20 years have passed. They can be small moments from your childhood that stick with you for one reason or another, or the big ones: your wedding day, the birth of your children.

I remember the day Jordan's mother, Tonya, and I found out she was pregnant. It was a hot day in July of 1998, and we took two tests in a row to make sure we read the little stick correctly. I was elated about having a child, and while I wanted a son, like any parent, I just wanted a healthy baby.

I was 30 years old, had been clean and sober for over five years, and was ready to embrace fatherhood head on. I couldn't have picked a better human being to raise a child with. As Tonya and I sat there, faced with the realization that we were bringing a child into the world. I remember feeling that this was my *opportunity* to give my child the tools he needed to make better choices than I did. To make sure that I did things right this time around.

I wanted to give him a childhood that would help shape him into a successful, well-rounded person who was better than me—because I knew what the alternative looked like. I wanted to teach him lessons that would stick with him as he grew into a man, lessons that would help put his life on a trajectory for success and far away from the path I had carved out for myself.

When I was five years old, my mother started taking me to the Maryland Penitentiary. It was one of those defining moments that sticks with a kid. My older cousin, Rob, found himself incarcerated there as a young man. We shared the same habit of poor decision making, and he had serious time to do for it.

I remember going to see him in the visiting room. It had a long, wooden horseshoe-shaped table in the middle. The inmates would file in from the basement, one by one, and sit on the inside of the shoe. Inmate on one side, visitors on the other.

Twenty years later, I found myself in that same inmate line. Shuffling up from the basement and sitting on the wrong side of that same table. The very first day, I was amazed that the room looked exactly as it did two decades before. But here I was, a 25-year-old man, back in the same spot my mother wanted me to avoid.

Is this what I want out of my life?

Right then, I felt that I was better than all of this. I realized at that moment I had been imprisoned mentally since my innocence was stolen from me at age five. I purchased my one-way ticket to prison at age 13. I wasn't going to be happy until I physically got here. Right *here* in this same place I was all of those years ago. That exact moment is when I got out of the prison of my mind. I had to physically come to one prison to mentally get out of another one. Now I had to put a plan together to stay out of both.

There are two ways to serve a prison sentence; either you do your bid, or you let your bid do you. I chose to do my bid by enrolling into a substance abuse treatment program. I began mastering mundane mental and physical routines to use when I got back into society. I was growing up as a man. It was then that I realized what a burden I had been to the people around me, and more specifically to the two people in the world who cared about me the most: my mother and Tonya.

I had put them through Hell, but I was glad that they both stood by me as much as they could. They were my supporters through this all, and two of the people who would come in and sit on the other side of that giant horseshoe table for me.

Once I got to State Pen, I knew it was up to me to persevere from this point moving forward. Tonya and my mother had buoyed me along to this point, but I needed to make lasting change for myself. My mind was made up. My plan was in motion, and I decided while I was incarcerated, I

23

had to take responsibility for my actions. I had done enough sharecropping and cotton picking for the systematic police, judicial and penal systems. I had to sign my own freedom papers.

I never realized the leadership skillset that I possessed at that time. I was never a total idiot. My poor decision making and the need to fit in always distorted my thoughts. I never realized that I gave myself a survival command at such a young age that would influence my way of thinking for years to come. I was molested by a babysitter, by someone who was supposed to be looking out for me, at such a young age. To cope, I gave myself one simple command to survive: "protect yourself at all times." And that is what I thought I had to do growing up.

My mother would always tell me that she could put me in a classroom of kids from the second grade on and I would always gravitate to the bad kids. The bad kids were probably hurt like me, but no one was messing with them. Every miscreant, sociopath, gangster, and nefarious individual I've instinctively ever hung with was just like me. Our behavior ensured that whoever failed us in our lives would never do that again. We hung with each other for protection. But now it was time for me to start taking care of myself.

My Inner Child

Tonya and I had been together for seven years before Jordan was born on March 3, 1999. Tonya had pregnancy complications due to an incompetent cervix. It required surgery, months of bedrest and it meant she couldn't carry Jordan to term.

As a first-time dad, having a premature baby is unbelievably overwhelming. You feel helpless, panicked, uncertain. I thought my poor decision making and experimentation in my younger days played a part in her complications. It's a natural fear to feel as though your baby may be limited physically, or worse, especially when they're born premature. Who knew that this 6lb 7oz, 21-inch baby who was so tiny, and "premature" would make such an impact, not only in my little corner of the universe, but across the world?

For the first three months of Jordan's life, I was intensely overprotective of him. Tonya and I both had to go back to work, so we decided to use a brand-new daycare provider who also happened to be one of Tonya's nurses at the hospital. The idea of trusting another human being with your child can nearly rip your heart out.

I'll admit, it took me a minute to get comfortable with anyone besides family looking after Jordan. But after weeks in the hospital, Tonya had developed a relationship with this nurse that ran the daycare, so off he went. Trust me when I say, if I could have stayed home and cared for him, I probably would have. And although I *trusted* his daycare, it didn't stop me from dropping in unannounced all the time to check in on him.

I wanted nothing more than to protect him in any way I could. To shelter him from any pain someone else could inflict on him. Because I understood what pain can do to a child.

One day, in my substance abuse treatment group at State Pen, a few months into my sentence, we started an exercise about our "inner child." I had to talk to my inner child about the pain that he experienced at such a young age. As I sat there, engaged in the exercise, all I could feel was shame. I was so ashamed that someone had failed me. Living with the fact that this happened to me fueled my anger, my behavior, my rebellion, and every other self-destructive feeling imaginable.

Did I bring this on myself?
Was it my fault?
How did I let this happen to me?
Is there something wrong with me?

These thoughts were constantly racing through my head, and I didn't have the tools to let what happened in the past stay there. This failure was with me daily until I did the work internally to let *my* inner child and my 6-year-old-self know that it wasn't my fault. This person was an adult. I was child.

It was your mother who failed you by unknowingly putting you in the care of a predator. A predator who had probably been failed by someone else along the way.

I had to apologize to my inner child for letting that happen to him. I had to explain that it wasn't his fault. That bad things happen to good people sometimes. Most of all, I assured him that I would never let anyone hurt him again. It is the same type of protective instinct that kicks in when you're a father and the one that makes you want to protect your poor, defenseless child at any cost.

And just like that, a thousand-pound weight of psychological despair, of guilt and shame, the weight I'd been carrying for the last 20 years, evaporated into thin air. I was getting my freedom from something I was ashamed to talk about for two decades, in prison of all places. Here I was, locked up inside of the Maryland State Penitentiary, yet I had never felt so free.

You are taught to leave your feelings at home when you go to prison. Feelings have no place there. Getting in tune with the way I felt helped my process. In prison, I chose not to numb the way I felt for so many years. I had to look my feelings in the eye and deal with them head on. And part of this meant getting involved in Narcotics Anonymous, or NA. Every Friday night while everyone else watched movies, I was at a NA meeting, listening to recovering addicts from the outside share their stories of hope and the reality of living clean.

My story now included my honesty about being sexually molested as a child and accepting that it wasn't my fault. Acceptance and forgiveness give freedom to the person who carries that type of shame around for so long. Here I am, in prison, sharing my story with my fellow inmates, not caring what they thought about me.

I had established respect from being Inmate Council President of that prison and for holding a few other inmate leadership positions. After the meeting that evening, three fellow inmates personally came up to me and told me about similar experiences, but they weren't ready to share them out loud.

"Marty, that happened to me too. I'm not ready to share it with the world like you just did."

They weren't at the place of acceptance and freedom that I had gotten to. The statistics of young boys that have been sexually molested are realistically staggering. The psychological trauma is acted out in so many ways. Most boys are taught early on "be tough," "don't cry," and the lifelong effects of that can go in so many directions.

I was crying for help with my behavior, but no one noticed. I clearly was not going through the normal "rebellious" stage. I was in pain and didn't know how to tell anyone. My mother never asked me if anyone touched me, my parents didn't ask if something was wrong. So, I stayed tough.

I often wonder out of those three guys, how many of them continued to stay on the hamster wheel of recidivism, in and out of prison. I wonder if they remained restrained by the psychological shackles that held them in prison of their minds, or if any of them broke free.

I remember one day, not long after this, standing in the prison yard with some of my fellow inmates. We were all young, in our mid-20s. Everyone was talking about their plans when they reentered society again. One guy was going back to work a job, two were going to make another attempt at selling drugs. My response was that my recovery was my only priority.

"As long as I don't use everything would come together."

Living Vicariously

I was asked more than a few times over the years, if I ever felt that I was living vicariously through Jordan. I'd always reply, "No, I never wanted to play football."

However, at the end of the day, I *was* living vicariously through my son, for practically his entire life. I wanted nothing but success for him in whatever he wanted to do.

My job as a father was to shape and mold him the way I wished someone had shaped and molded me. It was my job to motivate, encourage, and support him to push to his maximum potential to pursue his dreams and aspirations. Jordan wanted to get a degree in Kinesiology and go to the NFL. I was confident he was on his way to making both a reality.

If he wanted to chase his dream and go pro after he got his degree, I'd be there to support him and push him mentally to do what was necessary to make it happen. I wanted him to have all the experiences he deserved and to truly enjoy a well-rounded life.

I wanted him to experience more of high school and college than just being a jock. From day one, I always encouraged him to make friends with everyone, not just athletes. I encouraged him to join other social clubs in high school to become more rounded. I encouraged him to be friends with everyone, so he'd never have to fit in with anyone.

I know how important it is to surround yourself with people from different walks of life, because you're a different person, whether good or bad, around friends. Just when we as parents think we know our children; we often find we don't know this other side of them and who they are to their friends.

I was beyond words when I heard from one of Jordan's close friends that everyone respected his musical ear. It wasn't a side of him I knew. I was beyond proud when I heard how much they respected him for how focused he was to get to the next level, that his peers, not just his parents, saw this. While some of his friends were en route for a senior weekend after graduation, Jordan was training for spring conditioning. He had friends who respected that side of him and encouraged it, instead of trying to stifle it.

I was surprised to find that he spoke more around his friends than he did around his mother and me. We always assumed he was a man of few words, like most kids today. We always had to ask definitive questions to get more than the customary one-line answers. Just like every parent, we had to follow him on social media to see his real feelings towards us and towards his life. He would share with the world how much he loved us and how he was feeling, even when he was the strong and silent type at home.

But he had people around him. People he talked to and shared other parts of his life with. If there was one trick in my parenting playbook that I knew I could use, it was my experience in knowing the power of surrounding yourself with the right people.

After I had completed my sentence with the state, I still had to pay the piper on that year-long suspended sentence. I'd gotten into a comfortable routine while in the Pen. I was Inmate Council President, the Recreation Commissioner, the NA/AA Chairperson and I was always in a self-help group. All things to make my time go by quickly.

In my own way, I was thriving in this environment, and going back to pre-trial jail where I started, wasn't going to work. The mentality and toxic behavior of people just coming in off the streets wasn't something I wanted to deal with.

In prison, you settle into communities of your peers and with people who have similar interests and mindsets. I'd made some good relationships with dudes that were trying to figure it out, just like I was. You choose your friends carefully in prison. Instinctively, I always hung with older people, and despite the age gap, my maturity level was never questioned. One of my good friends and mentors to this day was someone I met in prison. We were walking buddies. We would walk the yard together talking politics, a cure for cancer, telling our funny stories, and most importantly, how to be successful once we reentered society again.

I must have written the judge who sentenced me to that one-year suspended sentence five different times begging him to let me serve the remaining year in the state system where I was. The pen is mightier than the sword if you have any writing skills. As an inmate, everything is a written request in a system where everyone wants their crisis to be the administration's emergency. I wrote and I wrote, pleading my case. Then, one day, the judge finally wrote back.

"You're going to the Baltimore County Detention Center to serve your sentence son, stop writing me."

If you're committed to serve a sentence in the county jail, more than likely you're going to work inside the jail as a floor worker or as kitchen worker. I was in a working man's housing unit as a floor worker, meaning my job was to take cleaning supplies and equipment to all the other units on that floor and clean the community showers.

Most of the time, you go to units talking to guys you know, passing messages and contraband. I never got caught up in the passing of cigarettes or anything else. I had only 5-7 months left. I was too close to the door to get caught up in something that wasn't worth it. I had put together my plan and was executing it so I could be successful once I touched down.

Prison is such a temperamental environment and people's emotions can go in so many different directions. The closer you are to the door, the better it is to strategically distance yourself from some of the social engagements that would normally otherwise fill your day. Playing sports, cards, chess, or checkers can erupt for no reason other than someone having a bad day—which can have untimely consequences when you're about to go home. I was in a routine of going to work and learning Spanish from my cellmate. I kept to myself and stayed focused on my recovery. I had even been promoted to the second floor which was the hub of the jail.

Everything from intake, classification, receiving, the infirmary, counselor's office, medical section and the day to day operations all happened on the second floor. I was able to see everyone who was coming into the jail, who was going to court, and who was being released. One day, I saw a guy named Ben who I was friends with in the Pen. We attended NA and a lot of substance abuse treatment groups together. He was actually the jailhouse reverend. Reverend Ben and I even did some of my NA step work in the yard. We had a fairly good relationship, just two cats trying to get it together to be successful upon our release.

Ben went home before I did, and one day as I was sitting in my broom closet office on the second floor, I saw him walking down the hall with some new prisoners. He hung his head down when he saw me. I asked him point blank what happened. *He had a plan for success.* He told me he does better in prison than he does in the streets.

I was devastated. Ben, like so many others, statistically does better in structured environments. Unfortunately, for guys like him, prison is one of those structured spaces.

Whenever recovering addicts from the outside would visit us during those Friday night meetings, they would always say to those of us in that NA meeting that "only two of you all are going to make it." I always told myself, I was one of those two. I still think about Reverend Ben and wonder if he ever became one of those two who made it as well.

A 2% success rate is a staggering number. I own a residential substance abuse and behavioral health treatment facility in Baltimore City. I would like to say our success numbers are higher than that, but they're not too far off.

Seeing so many things about the judicial and prison system on that second floor gave me a lot to think about. Seeing my friend Ben and so many other guys get released on a Friday and then come back that Monday or Tuesday, made me fear what I was up against when I returned to society. My recovery was my first priority and I was willing and receptive to do everything suggested to be successful at it.

I had made a few friendships with correctional officers while I was at the Baltimore County Detention Center. One was Officer Greg, who didn't mind lending his reading materials to inmates. His books about mental slavery, systematic imprisonment and the plight of the black man in America had motivated me to write about my experiences.

Then, there was Officer Edward Norris, a maintenance officer at the jail. One day, Officer Ed asked me if I'd read the autobiography of Malcolm X. I said I was familiar with it. It was actually one of the books I had in my cell as a part of my reading collection. He also asked me what I was doing here. Not what got me here, but what *I was doing* in the present moment to better my situation.

Ed told me that Officer Greg had showed him some of my writings. Then he said, "I want a brother like you to raise my son if something ever happens to me." I didn't know how to respond to that, I was in the process of finding my way in life. I was trying to grow up as a man myself. Clearly, Ed saw my potential at a time when I couldn't see it myself.

Later that day, back in my cell I began to read the *Autobiography of Malcolm X*, but I began wondering what Officer Norris' angle was. My mind was still small at the time.

Was he gay?
Was he trying to bite at me?

In those days, I was only starting to open up to different sources of information. If you didn't talk like me or look like me, I had a problem listening to you.

Why would this guy want me to raise his son if something happened to him?
He doesn't even know me.

One day, I casually mentioned I was focused on my recovery and going home. He stepped away, came back and whispered to me that he just celebrated his eighth year of clean time. Right then, I saw a higher power working in my. I asked him to be my very first sponsor. I was really opening up to receiving information from other recovering addicts. You could've been a green space Martian, but if you had more clean time than me, I was going to listen to what you had to say.

If there is one piece of advice I would give recovering addicts once they are released from a treatment facility, jail, or prison, it would be this: go straight to a meeting, raise your hand and let someone know you just got released. Don't go to your mom's house, or your girlfriend's house, go get something to eat, take your ass straight to a meeting and raise your hand.

After five months, some odd days and a few hours in the Baltimore County Detention Center, I was a free man, both mentally and physically. I wasn't anxious or scared because I'd already had a plan in place, and I knew it was up to me to execute it. I was released from the county detention center in June 1997 and never returned.

My friend and first sponsor, Officer Ed, picked me up that day in his little beat up stick shift Honda Accord. I reached for the radio. I hadn't heard any real music in months and Ed's radio didn't work. I let out a hearty laugh. We could've been on a scooter, I didn't care. I was just grateful to have the sun on my face and to finally see some daylight. Ed drove me straight to a marathon meeting where I saw several familiar faces of guys who came behind the wall to bring some hope and inspiration to us in NA.

I raised my hand that day and said, "I'm Marty, I'm a grateful recovering addict. I just got released today. I want a new way of life."

Ed continued to play a significant role in my life. He always told me I had the answers to my own questions whenever I asked his input or advice on something. He taught me a lot about coping skills. When you don't have an option to escape from your problems, you strengthen your ability to cope with life happening.

In recovery, there is a saying, "life gets good; life gets better and then life gets real." I was learning to deal with real adversity. I'd been addicted and incarcerated, all the things the average person is afraid of. I'd learned to deal with life head on and tackled so many hurdles. I truly thought I had been through it all—and that it had prepared me for the worst that life could throw at me. But I was wrong. Unfortunately, my most challenging moment would come decades later, when I lost my most precious gift, Jordan.

Ed helped me in more ways than one. He was at Tonya's baby shower and every one of Jordan's birthday parties. He was such a presence in our lives until he passed away after a long battle with pancreatic cancer. His son, Omari, was a teenager when he passed. We lost touch for some years, and then I saw him one day in Dunkin Donuts and told him about the conversation Ed and I had when we first met. Omari was too old for me to raise him, he had a family of his own, but I wanted to help. Then he asked me to teach him how to drive. It was such a simple thing, and one I was honored to do.

As I think back about it, prison was one of the best things to happen to me at that time in my life. The opportunity to grow mentally and release all my psychological and traumatic baggage allowed me to finally enter the right of passage into manhood as the man I was supposed to be.

My successful re-entry plan consisted of continuing to practice the mundane habits I had made a part of my routine in prison. I followed all the suggestions my predecessors in NA suggested. I saw what the right guidance could do for me.

While I was gone, I realized no matter how much my mother loved me, she was my biggest enabler. I was prepared to reside anywhere other than back at her home. So, I moved in with Tonya. The three most important things you need to successfully reenter into society are: housing, mental health support and substance abuse support. I had a place to live, I didn't feel that I had any mental health challenges and I definitely was passionate about my recovery.

While finding my way early on in the NA community, I would attend meetings the majority of the day. I still was searching for my own identity like so many people early in recovery. I found friends through NA and my sponsor, Ed, even found me a part time job with a cleaning company. I cleaned two properties, a luxury apartment building in South East Baltimore and a church in Baltimore County. I laugh now, because I would be jumping out of my skin a lot of nights in that church. I wasn't scared of anything while I was inside, yet I was terrified alone in that church. But it didn't matter. I was out and I was moving forward with my life.

Tonya and I created a real partnership then. We had been through my bad times early on, but I'm glad we went through those things before we had Jordan. Tonya's sagacity during my sentence is what kept me grounded. I was in my process of learning to grow up and take accountability for my actions and decisions. I was right where I was supposed to be in my life. I'm just grateful that I got it together at an early age.

I had been released from prison, physically and mentally, and was trying to find my place and purpose in the world. I was confident that if I completed a prison sentence, I could do anything that I put my mind to. My successes after release were slow and incremental. One job led to a better job. My first car always broke down near payday, until I got a better car. I enrolled in different training courses in different careers, and as I accumulated more clean time, life got better.

It didn't happen overnight. I've always been a serial entrepreneur, so I was never afraid to try a new business. The challenges of reentry were complex and frustrating at times.

Whenever I would fill out a job application, there was always that little box at the end of the form.

Have you ever been convicted?

I'd check the box and the explanation began. Depending how heartfelt your explanation was, and what verbiage you used to explain it, you may have gotten hired. But more often than not, that check mark was a major red light.

I realized that I could create my own lane where I didn't have to explain anything to anyone regarding my potential for success. And slowly, but surely, it led me to where I am now. Over 20 years later, I co-own a substance abuse program, just two blocks away from the first meeting I attended after prison. I was a client and now I am the president, and truly able to relate to every individual who walks through our doors in their fight with the disease of addiction.

When I became a father, I was confident about my role in my son's life. I had so many life experiences under my belt. I had as much of a perspective on *what to do* as I did with *what not to do*. Everything I had gone through to get to that point in my life was helping to shape me towards something so much more important than being a prisoner, an entrepreneur, or even a recovering addict—it was helping shape me towards being a father.

PART II

Finding a Niche

From the time Jordan ever played his first game of flag football at 6 years old, I knew he had a certain affinity for sports. Even as a kid, he was always a team player. I suppose it had a lot to do with his gentle, kind nature. I, like most fathers, wanted him to become a superior athlete, but I knew that the social nutrition of sports would make him a well-rounded young man.

Back then, Jordan's life-long friend, future teammate and mentor, Ellis, was the flag football team's quarterback. Even at the age of 6, Jordan was so much bigger than Ellis and pretty much any kid he came across. When the majority of his teammates from flag went on to play tackle football with pads, Jordan significantly outweighed them.

He was too big to play with the guys his age. Most leagues had a weight limit on them—and Jordan didn't make the cut.

Growing up, Jordan was always the tallest guy in his class, I believe his quiet demeanor always came from him not wanting to draw extra attention to himself, especially when he was younger. When you're at that vulnerable age, and trying to find your identity, extra attention isn't always a good thing.

We didn't know of any unlimited weight football leagues at the time, so we transitioned into playing baseball and basketball. Jordan sucked at baseball, or perhaps it was that I didn't have the patience of watching him in the outfield doing nothing. He did seem to find his place on the basketball court as a big man. I still remember the little sports card picture of him in his basketball uniform with his two front teeth missing and that big smile that seemed to cover his entire face. It still makes me laugh every time I envision it. Who knew that sports would be his niche in life?

When Tonya was pregnant, we had a friend we called "the Prophet," because he had the gift of sight. The Prophet told Tonya that Jordan would be born with asthma, but that he would grow out of. He also said he would excel in some type of sport, baseball or basketball.

As the Prophet called it, Jordan was born with asthma, which he grew out of by the time he was four years old. This made me feel as though I had some insider information regarding his sports skillset, and what he was about to be. And I, like most fathers, wanted to expose it. I wanted him to be a superstar on the court by age eight.

I always envisioned Jordan playing basketball. I never considered football. He was finally finding his place in basketball and finding acceptance. The only problem was, he was growing so fast that we had to get his mental capabilities caught up with his physical ones.

Jordan and I would play basketball most Sundays and I'd always play him as aggressive and tough as I could—beating him up on every play. He would play me hard one-on-one, however he would never play the opposing team his age the way he played me. He was the definition of a gentle giant. You really had to rattle his chain to get him to play emotionally. I used to try to motivate him as much as possible.

"Just imagine you're out there playing against me."

As much as I tried, it never worked, until he started playing football.

When Jordan was in middle school, he was playing AAU basketball and middle school basketball. After the games, a coach by the name of Bill Rogers, would come and ask me if we had thought about football. I'd say, "No coach, Jordan is a basketball player." And he would say, "Mr. McNair Jordan is a lineman." He wore me down and kept asking. Then finally, he convinced me to speak to some other coaches from the Hamilton Tigers Unlimited program.

The first time one of the coaches from Hamilton came out to the house to speak with us, he had another player with him. For the first time in Jordan's 13 years of life, he saw someone his age that was bigger than him. Tonya and I kept looking at each other in amazement at the size of "Big Al." We always thought Jordan was the biggest kid on the block.

Shocked, I immediately told Jordan to give Big Al a few pairs of sneakers. People were always passing down big sneakers to Jordan, since we could never find them in most stores—and we had never met someone big enough to pay it forward to. Between Big Al and the coach, Tonya and I were sold on football, now I just had to convince Jordan to give football a try.

Jordan would never admit to it, but he tried to wiggle out of football practice at first. One time, he tried to convince me to take him to see the Crime Stopper instead of going to practice. The Crime Stopper was this basketball phenom in Baltimore City by the name of Khalil Carr. He got this moniker because the crime rate in Baltimore would go down when he was playing. Every time he stepped on the court, everyone would want to watch him play instead of going out and getting in trouble. At the time, for Jordan, watching basketball was still more important than getting on the football field.

I convinced him to try football for a month with my famous "we're McNairs, were good at whatever we put our minds to," speech. Jordan didn't know a thing about football. However, once he got to practice, he noticed he was quicker than his other teammates on the line. His basketball feet were working in his favor, and even though he hadn't been playing as long as some of his teammates, he had an edge that they didn't.

When Jordan reached the 8th grade, a lot of schools were recruiting from the Hamilton program. Their relationships with various private schools in the Maryland and DC area gave their student athletes the opportunity to attend better academic institutions. Jordan was recruited by quite a few and was ultimately accepted into the McDonogh School as a Foundation's Program recipient. Tonya and I were thrilled, as McDonogh isn't just one of the area's leading private schools, but it was only about 15 minutes from home.

The school offered a bridge program to help get incoming students caught up to speed academically with the private school curriculum. It even included tutoring and athletic training. I knew it was a real opportunity for Jordan to grow not only on the field but in the classroom.

Jordan changed so much at that school. He truly began developing not only into a scholar and an athlete—but a great human being as well. He has access to athletic training. He had an offensive line coach, Spencer Fallaou, who played professionally with the Baltimore Ravens. His mentors, coaches and teachers all saw potential in Jordan and were vested in his success. I knew how much I needed that as a young person and was thrilled that Jordan had the right support around him.

Even when Jordan was diagnosed with ADHD his freshman year, he embraced it and developed an even stronger work ethic. I would take him to school early before the day started and he would work with his teachers on his studies or exams. He had one teacher in particular who promised to get him NCAA eligible because she knew of his potential for the next level. Jordan had a particular fondness for Latin, which I didn't understand because he never spoke a word to me whenever I ask him about it. But his dedicated work ethic in the classroom and on the field was shaping in him into a young man that I couldn't be prouder of.

While Jordan was navigating his way through high school, offers from colleges started coming in, as early as his freshman year. He'd received multiple offers from Maryland, Ohio State, Notre Dame, Penn State, and Alabama, all to play football. It was exciting but we never wanted him to get too ahead of himself. One day, Tonya and I had a come to Jesus talk with him and we let him know "We don't care how many offers you've received Mr. Big Man. You need to study harder in Algebra, now go take the trash out."

We decided early on to keep Jordan grounded no matter how many offers he received. He needed to graduate first. I was still the proud father every time I got a text letting me know a new school made him an offer. I knew he was confident in his playing ability to play at a big college program and that it would open doors, not only for football but for him to get a great education.

Many of Jordan's offers were coming in because of his size and raw athletic potential. But I knew that he still needed to bring in the mental part of his game. Finally, when he was 15 years old—it just clicked. Jordan was playing basketball and football at McDonogh. He would still play the occasional AAU basketball game on the weekends in exchange for a free pair of sneakers. There weren't too many big men that wore a size 15 shoe at 15 years old, so it was win-win.

That weekend he was playing in Pennsylvania with a team from Baltimore against a team from New Jersey. This older looking kid kept talking trash to Jordan the whole game, really trying to intimidate him. That same kid caught a fast break and Jordan trailed him and assaulted him with hardest legal foul I've seen since the Detroit Pistons played the Chicago Bulls in the 1990s.

I'd never seen that switch turn on like that. I had never seen him use his size to his advantage. "Finally, he's got it," I said to myself as I beamed with joy. My son, who has had this ability with the strength and size to do this all along, finally stood up for himself. The kid jumped up ready to fight, Jordan was more than ready to defend himself. The kid's parents were sitting next to me in the stands. They said something, I said something, a typical day in the stands with emotional parents at a sporting event.

As I moved to sit in another section, I was beaming with pride. I knew he needed to have more intensity on the field to make it to the next level.

He finally got it, not when I wanted to, but when he was ready to, and it couldn't have made me happier.

Building Momentum

Being a father can be both rewarding and humbling. The expectations of wanting your child to be better than you or more successful than you can be all-consuming. We sacrifice so many things for our children's success and it is always our fault when things don't go according to plan. We do all we can, and at times they feel we still could have done more.

We still encourage our children when life teaches them the lesson that we taught first, as if we didn't know how'd that chapter of their experiences would end. We receive the corniest of gifts on Father's Day and we beam with joy that one day out of the year someone thought of us. I still have the three-ball golf ball set with DAD spelled out on my desk from Jordan.

However, the best gift of all was every time he would have his own success in his life, no matter how big or small. Just to be a part of it and to have a hand in it was truly rewarding.

By the time Jordan was a sophomore, I was seeing him come into his own as an athlete, and realizing this dream of his to play at the next level wasn't just a dream, it was something very real and obtainable. He was seeing the results of his own hard work and the impact that it made not only on his own physical prowess, but on his team.

That year, Jordan's team, the McDonagh Eagles traveled to Cincinnati, Ohio to play a team known as the Elder Panthers. The Panthers were a powerhouse team with 99 players on their roster, and this was an opportunity for Jordan's squad to play a team completely outside of their MIAA conference. The average player on this team was six feet or taller—a tough matchup for our McDonogh Eagles, but it was an exciting challenge.

I still remember the ride to Cincinnati and being wrought with anxiety. As we finally arrived after a long seven-hour journey, the Elder fans were so welcoming, they even tailgated with us in the parking lot of the school before the game. While they were extremely hospitable, they kept talking to us as if we didn't know what were in for, driving up all this way for a loss.

Elder's football stadium is affectionately known as The Pit. It's an old stadium, started in the 1930's by student and parent volunteers, and ultimately completed in 1947 after WWII. It seats 10,000 fans and is known for drawing some of the largest high school football crowds in the country. The fanbase has been compared to the Cubs fanbase at Wrigley Field.

It wasn't like anything these high school kids had seen before. It's a horseshoe shaped stadium, made entirely of concrete and dug into the side of a hill. It is beyond intimidating, even as a spectator. No wonder all the fans were so confident in their victory. Unfortunately for them, the final score that day was one of the biggest upsets the Panthers ever experienced. Jordan and the McDonogh Eagles rattled the Elder Panthers and every fan in Elder, Ohio with them. When the scoreboard lit up with the final 28-14 tally, you could hear a pin drop it was so quiet in that stadium.

Jordan played offensive tackle, a position many say is one of the most difficult to play at a higher level. You often hear people play lip service to the offensive lineman and talk about how "important" they are to the quarterback, but they are often misunderstood.

You don't just need to be big to be an offensive tackle. It takes a rare breed to master this position, it requires size and strength, yes, but you need more than just a 6'5", 300-pound frame. You need to be quick, have solid hands for that jarring blow to a defender and be extremely agile. Jordan's speed an agility never ceased to amaze me when he played. When most opposing teams saw Jordan, the first thing they noticed was his size, when he stepped on the field, it was always those quick basketball feet that left their jaws on the floor. I loved watching

Jordan on the field, loved seeing his agility—and how quickly he snapped into action at the start of a play.

That game was one of those moments where Jordan really got a taste of what sports at a higher level could be like. Of what playing in front of that many fans with that high of stakes could be like for his future. I'm confident that games like this are what pushed him towards wanting to make football his focus in life.

I would get so invested in these games and in my son's successes. But as parents, you don't just get to see your son win either, you get to see first-hand why sports are so important to young people. It was a great underdog story, yes, but it was one of those moments where I got to see my son have his own success in life. I knew that all those one-on-one games on Sundays, late practices, weekend road-trips and dragging him to football practice as a middle-schooler had all really paid off. It helped him find his passion.

The following year, as a junior, Jordan rocked my world when he told me he wanted to concentrate on football only. He said, "Dad, I've decided not to play basketball again." He saw where football could take him and wanted to hone his skills and really work on being an elite offensive lineman.

I was crushed to say the least. He had finally grasped hold of the enforcer mentality while on the football field, but he was always a great basketball player. I was so proud he finally learned how to use his size as a big man on the court. However, I saw the passion he had for football. I saw it in big games like the Elder one, and I saw it in his everyday routine, in the way he practiced, in his off-season training.

Football is the one sport where a big man can truly be a big man. I'd stop playing one on one with Jordan, it seemed the taller he got the shorter I got. We'd go at it aggressively on Sundays but ultimately, I was the only one who felt it Monday. I didn't need to toughen him up anymore. It was one of those lessons he finally got a hold of. He didn't need me to have a hand in that part of his life anyone. But while our Sunday lessons on the court came to an end, there was still plenty for me to teach my son.

The Next Level

Jordan was the most sought-after recruit his junior and senior year at the McDonogh School. On the first day of school Jordan's junior year there were literally 200 pieces of mail in the mailbox from different colleges. He would average 50 pieces of mail weekly for the remainder of the year.

The college courting process can be both the best and most stressful times of a high school athlete's life. Being bombarded with so many schools can be a good thing, but not receiving any offers can be equally as stressful. The recruitment mail is so entertainingly flattering to any young person looking to go to the next level, it's hard not to get a big head.

A Photo Shopped picture of Jordan walking through the crowd with the rest of the team towards a game. A doctored image of him celebrating with the school's fans. The photo of him in a cap and gown at graduation. And of course, there were the many photos of him in a school's helmet on the cover of *Sports Illustrated.*

It's surreal now thinking back on all of that recruitment mail, that he would be the most talked about student athlete of 2018 for a tragedy, instead of his successes. I thought those doctored photos were previews of the future life my son had in front of him. I had no idea that Jordan would never get the opportunity to have many of these manufactured experiences.

As the piles of recruitment materials continued fluttering in, Ohio State's letters kept making their way to the top. Jordan always wanted to go to Ohio State to play football. They even made him an offer while he was still a freshman, meaning they were interested in his raw athletic potential, as long as he continued to develop on the field. So, in January Jordan asked me to take him up to Ohio for a visit.

A lot had changed since the last road trip to Ohio when Jordan was a sophomore. At the time, I was in the process of adding the behavioral health and substance abuse program to my company's existing transitional housing program. Money was extremely tight all of 2015, and all of our financial resources went into staying afloat while we awaited licensure for the treatment facility.

When you're in that position as an entrepreneur, you have to sacrifice some things just to keep your head above water—and car insurance and medical insurance were on my list. One of my friends in the car business had to give me a sticker for my tags because they'd recently expired. It was a challenging time, but like most parents I did my best to protect my son from the direness of my financial situation.

Our drug treatment facility's opening was on the horizon, and we would be in the black soon enough. At that moment, I should not, technically speaking, have been driving. But I made a promise to my son and made the decision to drive Jordan up to Columbus, Ohio to visit the school of his dreams. I had suspended tags, little money, and no insurance, but there was no way I wasn't going to take him.

The process of choosing a college can be overwhelming for any student, but when you're a highly recruited student athlete, it's a completely different ballgame. All coaches start to sound like used car salesmen. You start trying to find any semblance of a symbiotic conversation, instead of just sitting through another sales pitch. The more schools you visit, the older it gets, and all of these talks and pitches start to blur together.

We visited quite a few schools that year, and you learn pretty quickly to start listening to what coaches are *saying* to you instead of what they are showing you. You have to stay focused on the message and try not to get blinded by the light of the championship rings or caught up by the number of student athletes that have made it to the NFL.

On top of that, you'll have to wade through statistics on student athlete graduation rates, the percentage of football players that got a degree and what perks and gifts they're going to give the team if they get to a bowl game. All this while you hope to figure one thing out: *where is the best place for my child?*

Before I could even make it to another one of these meetings, I had to make it to Ohio first. The drive through the mountains was agonizing. We journeyed along two-lane roads and through small towns with the local police waiting to pull over any out of state car they could. The whole drive had me sweating bullets inside. Jordan had recently gotten his driver's license and he kept asking me if he could drive, but I had to keep trying to play it cool.

We arrived intact at Ohio State. As I attempted to catch my breath from the stress of the drive in, Jordan was immediately on top on the world. He was elated to finally be outside the football building of his dream school. I was just happy we made it there in one piece. Then, instantly I found myself blinded by all of the diamonds from their championship rings on display. Ohio State was going to put on quite the show.

As we strolled through Ohio State's football facilities, we were met with pictures of the many alumni who have made it to the NFL. It's hard not to get caught up in the success of a powerhouse program like this and imagine your own son up on that wall. A lot of these schools know how to hit you with enough shine to get the parents' attention, as much as the athletes. I, like most parents, wanted to know about graduation rates and about available academic support—the things that I still felt were relevant to making a decision when the time came.

Jordan, like most kids, was focused on the connection to Lebron James and his shoe deal, the barbershop in the locker room, and the gift bag you'd receive when you beat Michigan, or as they called it—"The Team Up North."

Jordan and the other recruits were walking ahead of us during our entire tour all equally enthusiastic about the showmanship of the Ohio State experience. While in the education segment of the visit, I was sitting in the back of the lecture hall, trying to stay focused on the fact that Ohio State was a university, not just a place to play football. Jordan and the rest of the recruits left ahead of the parents, and I stepped out, in an attempt to catch up to him. That is when I was directed to head coach, Urban Meyer's office for a meeting.

When I arrived, Jordan was already sitting there waiting for me. It's a big deal when the head coach from a program personally sits down with you, especially when they're as highly regarded as Urban Meyer.

As we sat there, discussing Jordan's future, I vividly remember Coach Meyer saying one thing to me, "Mr. McNair, whether Jordan attends Ohio State or not, make sure he gets a lifetime scholarship wherever you decide to go. These schools will get everything they can out of your student athlete, make sure you do the same."

Coach Meyer's piece of advice resonated with me and put that at the forefront of our decision-making process moving forward.

When we left Urban Meyer's office, they whisked Jordan and I away in a black SUV to one of the most recognizable landmarks in all of college athletics, The Ohio Stadium. The stadium seats 102,780 fans and is the fourth largest on campus stadium in the nation. Since opening in 1922, more than 36 million fans have streamed through the stadium's portals.

Jordan and I walked through the tunnel that the Buckeyes ran out of every home game onto the field. It was exhilarating to stand in the middle of that stadium looking around at where Jordan's college football career could be played, knowing he could be a part of something that big.

While this grand moment stood out to both of us as we continued through the college visit process, there was something about the University of Maryland that kept pulling Jordan back in. We had been to Maryland, or UMD, on several occasions while Jordan was being recruited under head coach Randy Edsell.

Jordan and I were both college basketball fans, and every time the recruits would get an invite, we'd attend a game. At first, the opportunity to go to a basketball game was really one of the biggest appeals of Maryland. UMD wasn't at the top of our list of schools, but we both enjoyed the added perk of getting to catch a game.

When Jordan turned 18 in March of that year, I told him we could go anywhere for his birthday. Anywhere at all—just pick a spot. He wanted to go to Universal Studios of all places.

Not the beaches of Miami, or to Las Vegas, but Universal Studios in Orlando, Florida. I'd always encouraged him to enjoy being a kid and to enjoy his age, and he did a great job following those directions.

Between Jordan's love for cartoons, and my excitement over Harry Potter World, the trip was a win for us both. While we were grabbing lunch one day inside the park, a random stranger came up and started asking Jordan about his plans for college. It was an easy conversation, even among strangers, as Jordan's size alone screamed college athlete. Conversations like this, although common, reminded us both that we needed to make a decision for his future and about where the best place for him would be.

After Tonya and I each took him on several visits, Jordan finally told us he wanted to visit UMD again. I wasn't particularly interested in Maryland; I didn't even know who the head coach was at that time. He said they wanted us all to come down one Saturday.

As Tonya and Jordan picked me up one rainy morning in March, I welcomed the chance to ride in the back seat, caught up in my own thoughts. I thought that UMD wasn't even on our list—*why were we even going there that day?*

When we pulled on to campus, we immediately went to the Gossett Building—a curved brick structure adorned with while pillars and meant to serve as the central hub for the Maryland Terrapin's football program.

Today, there is a tree in memory of Jordan planted in front of the building, a small memorial to my son. Back then, it was just another building—another one of the many "field houses" on college campuses, ready to lure us in with flash and bling. Today, it serves as a type of memorial on campus, a reminder to staff, students and players of the tragedy that took place there.

As we were greeted by the coaching staff, I noticed that we were the only ones there. This wasn't the normal visit for multiple recruits, they were serious about Jordan. There were only two other recruits on campus that day and each of these kids were about to get Maryland's A game. As we all sat there, listening to a well-rehearsed speech from Maryland's educational advisor, we heard the words "lifetime scholarship."

Tonya and my eyes met from across the room, they instantly had our attention. Urban Meyer's words kept ringing in my head, and suddenly, Maryland was in the running.

A lifetime scholarship provides athletes with the ability to return to school and complete a degree anytime in their life. So, if a student went to the NFL or NBA before they graduated, they could come back to obtain their degree from that school when their professional career was over.

Even though we thought that wouldn't be Jordan's case and that he would graduate on time, it was still an incentive to influence our decision. We thought about the type of support he would get later in life, after college. We knew that being a

University of Maryland alumni could open up doors for jobs and networks in the area when football was done.

Jordan and I had visited the University of Maryland on several occasions, so we had been on campus before, but this day was different. I had never met this staff, we didn't know many of the faces before us, and I didn't know much about this new coach. The visit to any program is always an opportunity for a college to show you why they are the right program for your son. You hear the same things every time.

"This is why your child should develop his academic and athletic career here."
"These are all of the things that we do to get them prepared for life after college."
"We promise to build them up and take care of them."

This day was no different than any other song and dance we heard at other schools. When we made it to this new head coach's office, we were met by DJ Durkin. He was a young, energetic guy who made an impression on Jordan.

His sales pitch was simple; there was too much talent in the DC, Maryland, Virginia, or DMV, area to *not* stay at home and build a football dynasty. He then gave Jordan an analogy that set everything in motion.

"If the new Jordan sneakers dropped that weekend and they were in Baltimore and Philadelphia, where would you buy them?" Durkin asked.

To this day, I wonder how many recruits he mesmerized with that question. They all wore Jordan brand shoes. It was a no brainer, you would buy them in Baltimore, you would buy close to home. If you could build a winning team anywhere—why wouldn't you do it close to home? There was so much talent in the DMV, but local athletes weren't being recruited properly, DJ Durkin wanted to change that.

There were three monitors on the wall above the black leather couches in Coach Durkin's office. The monitors each had the NFL salaries of three positions: a left tackle, a quarterback and a defensive end.

That day, Jordan, a left tackle, Kasim Hill, a quarterback and Cam Spence, a defensive end, were all there for an intimate visit. They were all local kids and they all got the same speech in that office while looking up at those monitors with their future NFL salaries plastered on the screen.

Those three boys all made a pact to attend Maryland, and to start a movement of local recruits. Jordan begged me to attend UMD. He was sold and had completely bought into wanting to build that dynasty. He completely bought into this future that DJ Durkin was selling him.

I was still on the fence and wanted to visit a couple of schools down south. I wanted Jordan to visit the real powerhouse football programs like Auburn and Alabama who were interested in him. While I was sitting on the fence, more kids in the DMV were buying into the "buying your Jordan sneakers closest to home," spiel and choosing to stay local.

DJ Durkin and the University of Maryland had a great recruiting year that year, better than the years before. Four and five-star athletes like Jordan, Kasim Hill, Johnny Jordan, Cam Spence, Marcus Minor and other local guys in his recruiting class were all part of the *stay at home* movement. Jordan was no different than most recruits who just wanted to be part of something great. This is what he thought he was signing up for, an opportunity to be part of something great.

Our job as parents was to look beyond football and to how the rest of his life would be impacted after college. The DMV, if he decided to stay, would be filled with employment opportunities as a secondary plan if football didn't take him to the professional level. I, as a father, had to look at where he was wanted instead of where he'd be needed to play at school.

Jordan and I would always have the conversation after every visit. We'd discuss the pros and cons of every program.

How many players already had his position?
What state was the school in?
Would they initially play a local athlete over him?

And most importantly, we discussed if the chance to *build* a championship team would be more rewarding than joining a championship team that was already built.

It seemed that UMD was in the process of building something great. They wouldn't win a championship game Jordan's first year, but it was their goal to build, and to win more games than the previous season, again and again. The incremental steps of playing together, winning more games, developing character until you win a bowl game is the formula for building a championship team. It was hard work, but something any athlete could feel proud of, and it was something that Jordan wanted to be a part of. I could respect that as a parent.

Once I gave in and let Jordan commit to Maryland, he posted his decision on Twitter, as they all do, and his commitment instantly went viral. At the time, Jordan was ranked in the top 25 nationally for offensive linemen. A decision like this to go to a program like Maryland cultivated some buzz.

Most kids that are indecisive about their final decision to attend a school like to play the shell game with the hats on National Signing Day. They will have 3-4 hats of schools they are interested in, hover around between choices, and then ultimately put on the cap of the school they've chosen. It's a common song and dance, a sort of rite of passage into the world of Division 1 athletics. But Jordan thought he was sure.

I wanted him to be really confident in his decision and not just look at it emotionally, but to really look at the pros and cons of his choice. I wanted him to learn a life lesson from this recruitment experience. This was a major decision in his life, and I didn't want him to regret it.

Just three days after his verbal commitment, the University of Alabama was at McDonogh. Jordan texted me that day with his straight, to the point message "Alabama just offered." I was flattered beyond words when his high school coach texted me and said, "Alabama wants you to visit."

For most high school coaches, to get that call from Coach Nick Saban's staff is like a blessing from the football gods themselves. Everyone knows the chances of going to the league are much higher coming from a school like Alabama where they breed NFL players.

Some kids will change their mind and de-commit from schools they have verbally pledged to for a variety of reasons. This is called flipping. A lot of schools do this, and some are more successful at it then others. Alabama wanted us to flip, and they are normally quite good at it. After all, how could the University of Maryland stand up against a powerhouse like the famous Roll Tide? They could not, at least not on paper.

However, we raised Jordan to be a man of his word and wanted him to know that the integrity behind giving your word and keeping your word. So, even with an offer from Alabama on the table, I texted his high school coach back.

"Tell them thanks for the interest, but we've committed to UMD."

At the end of the day, the recruitment process all comes down to relationships. It's about the dynamic between the player and his family, with the recruiters and coaches that want him. Most families feel comfortable with the coach that recruits their student athlete. They feel as though this is *the person* that will look after them.

If it's a coach that you're comfortable with and that coach decides to take a job at another program, his recruit is going with him. That relationship is built on a mutual respect and understanding. They commit to looking after your child, and you commit to keeping your word to play for them.

College football is an interesting game, not only on the field, but with of all of the politics involved. Jordan made a commitment to come play for coach DJ Durkin at the University of Maryland—and we thought we had a commitment from a coach and a man to look after our son.

Jordan kept his side of the agreement, as a man should. He turned down offers from better programs and kept his commitment and his word to DJ Durkin. But Coach Durkin failed to hold up his end of the agreement.

After all the back and forth, the countless visits and the offers from other school, my son decided to be a man of his word. To play for a coach that wanted him to stay local, to build a legacy. It was big decision that Jordan thought would change his life for the better, to teach him how to build something from the ground up for DJ Durkin and the University of Maryland football program. But ultimately, it was a decision that was memorialized by a tree in a front of a football building.

The Senior Project

By the time Jordan was a senior, football was his top priority. However, he still had to keep up academically. One of his school projects required him to work at a local business for two weeks, and I was elated when he chose to come with work me.

I co-own a behavioral health and substance abuse program in Baltimore, and for two weeks, Jordan worked with my staff and wrote a report about what he did and what he learned.

Baltimore City can be everything that you hear and read about in the media. The statistics of addiction and violence are the reason we are a city in crisis. My program caters to men and women who found themselves in the same cycle I once did, and who are trying to get themselves together. Some for the first-time, others for the third, fourth or fifth time.

It isn't always easy trying to help people find their way, and Jordan knew that. I was proud that my son was choosing to spend his time here regardless.

I peeked in Jordan's notebook one day and was surprised by how many notes he was taking. He was *listening* to what was going on in those groups. One of the things that we discussed was these weren't bad people, but instead, that this is what a habit of consistent poor decision making looks like. This is where people who had followed the crowd wound up at after years of drug and alcohol use.

One day, in a group session, a young man, only a few years older than Jordan shared his story: drug use, incarceration and a close brush with death. To see this young man, who was the age of Jordan's older cousin was sobering; it really scared him in a way.

When Jordan was little, he was scared of everything. He would often grab my hand when he was scared and almost squeeze the blood out of it. I would always joke him as he got older how hard it was to believe Mr. "Big Ticket" athlete was scared of anything in a costume when he was a little boy.

It would have been a total waste of money to go to Disneyland in those days. He probably would not have even stepped foot in the park. Even at 6'5, 300 pounds he'd still opt out of going to haunted houses with me every year. Size aside, he still had that fear of the unknown inside him.

Jordan and I always spent our Sundays together, even after our one-one-one games ended. And one Sunday, while he was finishing his senior project, I told him he was working with *me* the following day and that he needed to wear some pants.

That morning, I never mentioned where we were going, or that we were in route to the Ordnance Road Correctional Center. I would often go to jails in the area to talk about our treatment program and assess potential clients upon their release, but it wasn't something I had ever shared with my son before.

My goal was to deter him from making poor decisions that could possibly lead to a place like this. I knew my redundant chant of "make good decisions" was one thing, but where was the proof to drive the point home?

I thought that this would be the best time to do it, since he was completing his project in my substance abuse facility. I wanted Jordan to see that all of this was an incremental type of behavior. You didn't just end up here or in my facility overnight. It was a product of bad decisions begetting bad decisions.

I knew that he was about to embark on his college career, and he would have to think on his own. I was confident that I'd given him enough raw information, however, he had to *see* where this behavior could send him: jails, institutions, or death. I knew, even at the time, this may have been a little extreme, I just wanted to let him see what I was so eager to experience at his age.

I never told him where we were going until we got to the jail, we had stopped by the Under Armour Outlet that morning to do some shopping. I casually asked him if he ever watched the show *Locked Up*. He said he had seen it a few times, but Jordan clearly didn't have an interest in that type of show. After all, that wasn't his reality. Jordan was a private school kid who realized as a rising freshman that his athletic potential could take him places in life. *Locked Up* did not have the same impact it would on me and my friends growing up.

It wasn't all that surprising. Jordan was never *that* private school guy, like a few of his friends were. The guy who wanted to emulate what the city kids were doing to look tough. A lot of his friends would sag their pants, showing off their underwear in some veiled attempt to look like the guys they would see in the inner cities. A "fashion statement" so to say.

Jordan was never that guy. He was the typical Sebago shoe, khakis, and blazer wearing student athlete. He had this one pair of Jordan's he bought, and no matter how disheveled they were he still wore them. It had gotten to the point I started to joke him about the state of his sneakers, but he didn't care. He was always comfortable in his own identity as a teenager. He found what style worked for him and he stuck to it.

That was Jordan. He was never impressionable like I was. Not with his sneakers, and for all I knew, not with his choices either. But I still wanted to subtly scare him straight and empower him at the same time, especially before he went to college. I wanted to give him firsthand information to stay on the right path to success. Something his peers didn't have, and something most kids his age never really come face to face with.

The interesting thing about jail and prison is we automatically think everyone inside is bad, that they inherently just are not *good people.* However, it is not *good* or *bad* that keeps these people inside. Many of them are stuck in these mental traps that keep the recidivism cycle constantly repeating itself.

The entire time Jordan was with me and doing his project, I would tell him that *these are good people*, but "this is what poor decision making looks like when you consistently do it."

When we arrived and started putting our valuables in a locker, 6'5, 300-pound Jordan was standing so close to me, I started to laugh. If he could have grabbed my hand, he probably would've at that moment. We had just gotten there, and my big man athlete was already scared of the unknown ahead.

Most of the guys in the group we met with that day all suffered from their own substance abuse challenges. That detention center is a low-level offense, co-ed jail. Most crimes committed by inmates are all drug related. As my son and I sat there listening to their stories, Jordan saw and heard the pain of these inmates who were unable get out of their own way.

The poor decision making of going back into the same communities upon release. The deaths within hours and days upon release from fentanyl overdoses. The coma one guy was in for two weeks after smoking K2, a synthetic marijuana.

The stories Jordan heard that day were impactful, even to me. These were all guys like him at one time in their lives. Young men who had an opportunity in life to make something of themselves, but who made more wrong decisions than right ones. And it led them here, locked behind bars.

As we sat and listened to these stories, I asked the question, I always do during these types of visits.

"Is this anyone's first incarceration?"

It wasn't.

When I asked if this was anyone's third to fifth incarceration, Jordan saw the honest hands raise as their eyes looked to the floor in embarrassment. Those groups are always genuine and gut-wrenchingly honest.

Those guys truly *wanted* help to stop their own cycle of recidivism, but few of them really would. Only about 2% of these men would be successful in their efforts. Out of the 40 guys that were in group that day, maybe one would stay clean.

When the group was over, Jordan got more handshakes and words of encouragement than he had probably ever received before. Everyone in the room wanted him to continue to be successful. Those guys who shared their stories could see the power of having a father as an example and one to guide you away from these decisions.

As we drove back from the detention center that day, Jordan sat deep in thought. It was sobering for him to see the real-life example of all of those lessons I taught him throughout the years.

It was hard for Jordan to see that, like him, and like so many young men, these guys also had promise and potential— they just didn't stay focused on utilizing it. We rode back in silence most of the way, but I knew he truly understood why I was always telling him to be cautious and why I wanted to make sure he didn't end up there.

Because anyone, even private-school student athletes can be a few poor decisions away from throwing all the promise and potential in the world away.

The Official Visit

Every student athlete has an official visit to the college campus that they've committed to. The "official visit" is financed by the school and is typically reserved for top recruits and their families. Getting asked is a huge step in a student athlete's recruiting journey.

This is when your student athlete gets to interact with their new, older teammates for the weekend, and when we as parents start looking at life on campus. As parents, we look at it as an opportunity for our children to make a good impression on their team and for the school to make a good impression on us. It is also an opportunity to ask ourselves "did we make the right decision by selecting this school?"

It is always a sigh of relief to settle on a program that you think you will be comfortable with. More than that, it is your child's first taste of the college experience. Essentially, this is the moment where you see if everything, or anything, that you've said along the way has been heard. This is the first test of many to see if they're going to follow the crowd or make their own choices when they head off on their own.

The day of Jordan's official visit, I asked him to come to my house first so we could ride together to the University of Maryland that evening. Tonya was meeting us there. We all had separate hotel rooms so he would be on his own while the coaches entertained and dined all the parents.

When he arrived at my house, I gave him an instant read urinalysis test. This is a test that is used randomly in my field to give an instant negative or positive reading for a laundry list of illicit substances. I told him to go pee in the cup and I explained the negative reading on all ten of the substances from marijuana to opiates. Yes, it was a scare tactic. But I wanted to get it in his head that he needed to start thinking more about every decision he made, particularly that weekend.

I reminded Jordan that he had more firsthand information than the average 18-year-old college freshman about poor decision making and where it could eventually lead to. He had an advantage, so to say, over other kids his age. It was up to him what he would do with that information. That weekend was one of his first real tests.

That evening, in route to UMD, we discussed his marching orders from the urinalysis results. I emphasized the fact that he should watch the people around him and watch the behaviors of the other recruits. I emphatically let Jordan know that there are three groups most student athletes fall into when they go off to college.

Group one would be leaders, the kids who are focused on doing what they have to do to graduate and get to the next level academically and professionally. These are the kids that know what they want to do and who they want to be, and they won't let anyone get in their way of making that happen.

The second group is the kids that have never been away from home, the kids who are easily influenced by peer pressure because they want to fit in. This group can go in either direction, because they're also looking for an identity, they just may not have the strength or the focus to get there.

The third group is the cool guys who party, drink and smoke weed and just want to fit in and give off a certain image. It will appear that they have it all together, but they don't. These are the kids who can easily start making all of the wrong decisions in life. "What group will you fall into, son?" I asked.

I told him to choose wisely, and that this trip was his first real opportunity to determine what group he would fall into when he started his college career.

"I'm confident that you personally have more information than the majority of your teammates."

I wanted him to watch who was smoking and drinking and to remember that he had no excuse for making poor decisions that weekend. If he made the wrong choice just to fit in, there was no other excuse besides the fact that he *wanted* to do it.

I left him with these words of wisdom, hoping they would be some of those fatherly anecdotes that actually sunk in. He got out of the car, and I let him know that I would need more urine Sunday when he got back home. If there were any positive results, there would be consequences. I would need his car back and life was be extremely challenging without a car.

I was a proud and confident father when I stopped by his hotel room Sunday morning. I felt my scare tactic had worked. Jordan was leader that weekend not a follower.

At first, it seemed like the University of Maryland was a great fit for Jordan. He was focused on his grades, he was hanging out with the right people and he was learning to take care of himself. He was even able to whip up some spaghetti for himself and his roommates.

Jordan was everything you expect from a college freshman. And he studied, all the time. Jordan wanted to get a degree in Kinesiology, and he knew that it would require making time for his schoolwork in between training and football.

Tonya and I loved having him close. It was easy to visit him, or pick him up for the weekend, and his whole family was around for home games. He made the traveling team as freshman, which we were all happy about. Jordan's first game as a Maryland Terrapin was against the Texas Longhorns on September 2, 2017.

Tonya and I didn't go to Texas for the season opener, but I invited a few people over to my friend Brian's house to watch the game. Brian has this cineplex style TV room in his house, outfitted with a massive flat screen, surround sound speakers, the works. It was the place we always watched big boxing matches and games—and now it was where I would be watching my son play college football on national television for the first time.

I was so excited to see Jordan in a Maryland uniform that Saturday, I almost couldn't sit still. I knew that this was not only his official debut into the world of college football, but his first step to hopefully play on Sundays in the future. I remember being so animated that day with every play. And in the fourth quarter, when Jordan finally got in the game for a few snaps, my heart started to beat faster and faster.

Do well, son.
Do a good job, son,
I'm proud of you son, way to go.

My son had beat the odds, he had avoided my past mistakes and he was making his television debut as Division 1 football player.

It was one of those moments where it all clicked, where I realized that the long days driving to games, the financial sacrifices and even the white-knuckle road trips without car insurance to Ohio State, had all lead to this one moment.

I was watching Jordan live his life to his fullest potential, doing something he loved. I couldn't help but think what about my own life and where I would be if I had the support system of a loving father. What heights would I have reached?

Any season opener win is always worthy of a celebration. The video footage of the Terrapins high-fiving with the Maryland fans after the game was priceless. Watching the close up of Jordan on TV giving the fans that victory fist bump was worth the price of admission that Saturday afternoon. I felt as though nothing could give me the feeling of euphoria I had at that moment. All was right with the world.

I couldn't wait to hear his version of the details. I remember asking him was he nervous about his first college game. He seemed so calm. What was he feeling?

"Dad, I was beyond nervous. The noise from the crowd was deafening."

Jordan was redshirted his freshman year, since the two linemen he was playing behind weren't injury prone but continued to be on the travel team. The coaching staff understandably decided not to waste his first year of eligibility. He did play in one other game that season, against nearby Towson University. And as his freshman year came to a end, Jordan set his sights on spring conditioning.

Spring conditioning typically starts at the end of May, right around Memorial Day weekend. Jordan was feeling confident. He had his first season under his belt, he was getting bigger, faster, stronger and he was ready to start training for the next season with a little more experience. He was poised to make more of an impact as a sophomore and he was ready to prove it on the field. Only none of us knew he would only make it to one day of training that year.

Selfies Along the Malecon

The weekend of May 25th, while visiting Cuba, I sent Jordan a selfie of myself and my Cuban friend Daykel along the Malecon. Internet is very limited in Cuba and Wi-Fi is usually only at the local hotels, so the process of sending pictures back home is rather complex. But I wanted to check in with my son, as I normally do when I travel, and I knew he was mentally gearing up to get back to practice and training.

Going to Cuba is like going back in time to the 1950's. The old cars, the little boys shooting marbles in the street, the little girls jumping rope, all living a life that seems so much slower and simpler than our lives here. It's not overrun with video games, Instagram and Snapchat or all of the other things that we Americans can't live without these days. It's like a completely different world down there, and a welcome reprieve from the stressful lives we all tend to live back home. It's always funny how different life 90 miles away from Ft Lauderdale can be.

My first visit to Cuba was with my then fiancé Dawn, in November of 2017. While awaiting our luggage to come off the conveyor belt in Cuba's tiny, cramped airport, I met an American-born Cuban kindred spirit named Naomi. We struck up a conversation and she made our first trip to Cuba a memorable one. Both of Naomi's families embraced Dawn and I on that trip.

We met them in a little one-bedroom apartment about 30 minutes from the heart of Old Havana. It was small, but warm and welcoming, and it even had its own Santeria altar. They instantly became family. We shared so many good times in that little apartment. My Spanish is limited but with Naomi's interpretation, it didn't matter. The language of laughter is universal.

During my second visit, Daykel and I walked into that small one-bedroom apartment on the other side of Havana bearing gifts; a pack of cigarettes for Luis Alberto and a bottle of Cuban Rum for whoever drank it. The first question they asked after embracing me was, "how are Jordan and Dawn?" Always the proud father, I had shown them so many pictures during our first visit. They were all amazed at Jordan's size and his enormous smile.

They had embraced him as their "grandè," or big nephew in America, with real dreams of playing in the NFL.

The language of support for our young people is equally understood. I let them know he was doing just fine; he was excited about football practice starting in a few days. I promised them that I'd bring him back with me the next time I visited.

Who would have known that while in Cuba, I was days away from life changing forever for all of us?

That selfie of Daykel and I laughing it up along the Malecon would be the last picture I ever sent to Jordan. I was so looking forward to sharing with Jordan the story of the two-peso meals I ate, riding the over-crowded buses, and of all that I had learned about Cuban culture.

Here I was, promising to bring Jordan back with me my next visit. A week later I was asking my Cuban family to pray for his life at that Santeria altar in their one-bedroom apartment.

PART III

May 28th, 2018

Tonya sent me a picture of Jordan the morning of May 28th. I had no idea it would be the last picture ever taken of him. His hair was cut extremely short, apparently due to a mishap with his barber. The only solution was to have it all cut off. He had been sporting the cruddy hair style like most of his friends did at the time. I was used to a full, uncombed, but shaped hair, that he could run his fingers through. But now it was gone. It was jarring at the time, seeing him look so different, but that is what kids do, they change.

Buzzed hair and all, I knew he was excited about practice starting. Jordan was a college coach's dream. A 19-year-old hardworking student athlete. A 6'5, 300-pound lineman that was quick on his feet. A kid recruited by nearly every top program out there, but who chose to stay home and build a program from the ground up.

Tonya and I had a good laugh about the new hair style. Our co-parenting partnership has always been from an organic place of genuine love and respect for one another. Our success in our relationship always came from one place: our love for Jordan. We realized early on in Jordan's life that we needed one another in order for our son to be successful.

We always worked to develop Jordan into a product of both of us, and into a human that was better than each of us alone. We never got caught up on who either of us were dating, if they wanted to join Team Jordan, we welcomed it.

Even when it came to disciplining Jordan, we always made sure we were on the same page. She supported me in my decisions, and I hers. A child should never see co-parents form a division. That is when they start to pick and play sides. There should always be a unified front, and that's what we always wanted to show Jordan, unwavering solidarity.

Tonya and I have been joined at the hip for a long time. Our relationship has evolved into an almost sibling-like partnership. Her fiancé, House, is a great man who helped us raise Jordan. Tonya *asked* my wife Dawn to please marry me. I'm an only child and her family has embraced me, my parents, my friends and anyone who I've ever brought around as one of their own. The example of love and support of growing together as a family has been significant in the way Tonya and I raised Jordan.

At times, Tonya and I would have the conversations about who would take Jordan back to school on the weekends. This was something I would never pass up, since she would pick him up on Fridays and bring him home. I always got stuck with the airfare when we traveled to away games. Who would pay car insurance since I bought his car? The typical things you discuss when co-parenting. She would always pull her infamous trump card "I feed him," which I never could really put up much of a fight against.

No matter what, we always worked together. The experience of going through this tragedy together continued to strengthen the bond that we already had. Once, when Jordan tore his pectoral muscle while in college, I remember meeting her at the school for MRI appointment. Jordan rarely got hurt and was never sick. So, any injury like this stuck out to us. But we always were there together, unified, whenever our son needed us to keep him safe.

The last thing I said to my son that day was "I know practice starts tomorrow, call me later this week." I had no idea my next conversation with him would be, "Son if you can hear me squeeze my finger. Son if you can hear me blink your eyes."

May 29th, 2018

"Mr. McNair this is an officer from UMD campus security, Jordan had a seizure at football practice this evening. We're at Washington Adventist Hospital Emergency Room, you should get here."

My world stopped.

I went to pick up Tonya. As we rode to the emergency room that evening, it felt like it did the year before, with Jordan's MRI. We were a unified front, going to make sure our son was safe. We were in it together. Unfortunately, we didn't know what was ahead. We had no idea what we were driving to and that our lives would forever change.

If there was a time when we needed each other's strength, this was it. I don't think we could've gotten through this without one another's love and support. We built a team over the last 19 years and sticking together was going to be the only way to make it through.

I tried to keep my composure until we got to the hospital, but I couldn't stop asking myself, "how could a 6'5, 300-pound kid who was as healthy as a horse and who had never been in the hospital before have a seizure?" The last time I saw him, he was healthy and vibrant, with that huge gap-toothed smile. And now had been rushed off the field and into the emergency room on the first day of practice. It just didn't make any sense.

When we arrived at Washington Adventist Emergency Room, we weren't prepared for what we saw. Jordan was in a cooling suit to get his body temperature down. There were two athletic trainers from the team there, and I immediately asked them if this type of injury had ever happened on one of their shifts before. The both said "no, it hadn't." When I think about how totally oblivious we were regarding heat-related injuries, it still makes my head spin.

I was the total optimist, thinking "he's 19 and strong, he'll recover quickly." How wrong I was. I knew nothing about this type of injury, or how serious it could really be. The cooling suit wasn't working. It wasn't getting Jordan's temperature down that evening. The next step was to induce a coma. We spent the night in the hospital still not knowing the magnitude of Jordan's injuries, or what was to come.

May 30th, 2018

That morning, Jordan's medical team made the decision to airlift him to the University of Maryland Shock Trauma Center in Baltimore City. The R. Adams Cowley Shock Trauma Center at the University of Maryland is the nation's first and only integrated trauma hospital. It is dedicated to treating the severely injured and employing groundbreaking research and innovative medical procedures with one goal in mind—saving lives.

I vividly remember one of the first doctors we spoke to in the Intensive Care Unit saying, "Your son is really sick." at least a dozen times in our initial conversation. In fact, I had to ask her to please stop saying it, we got the message.

That was Wednesday. The day after we found out our healthy 6'5, 300-pound, size-16-shoe child was fighting for his life. Jordan hadn't been in the hospital since he was born. He had a handful sports injuries along the way, like most kids do. Many of them were due to his body growing so fast. He had a few Achilles tears as an adolescent, needed that MRI a year before, but that was it. He had never really been sick. Unbeknownst to Tonya and me, the term "heat stroke" was much more serious than we ever thought.

We took it lightly. I always thought that a little heat stroke was just that. You stayed out in the sun too long and all you needed was some water in the shade to cool down.

As the crowd of supporters, teammates, coaches, athletic trainers, friends and family came to support us, we still didn't know what actually happened to Jordan. The coaches and everyone on the field May 29th knew, but Tonya and I didn't know anything. The athletic trainers, coaching staff and players knew exactly what got our son in this place, and his parents still knew nothing. We only knew that Jordan was now fighting for his life.

As the hundreds of supporters came to the hospital for Jordan, I initially thought that it was an outpouring of love for a teammate. I thought it was a supportive athletic and coaching staff. What I didn't know was that the two athletic trainers I had questioned just days before, the two trainers who were taking shifts by Jordan's bedside, were really to blame for this tragedy.

The doctors talked of a heat-related injury, and we began to learn about the impact the injury had on Jordan's liver. That Jordan really was extremely sick. That his organs were failing rapidly. As parents who are not medical doctors, it was hard to keep up with all of the terms they were using and the names of the machines that were keeping him alive. I could barely comprehend that we were here in the first place, let alone learn a new dictionary of medical terms.

Jordan was on kidney dialysis and an ECMO machine which pumps oxygenated blood through the body giving the heart and lungs a chance to rest. They also put him on a liver dialysis machine to help purify his blood after liver failure.

There was so much going on at the hospital between the rapid changes in his condition and the hundreds of visitors, family members, supporters, it became too much to process at once. While I appreciated the sentiment and the support, it was more overwhelming than anything.

I had to get out of that environment, clear my head and get information on what was really going on with my son, in a way I could process. Leaving the hospital that night, I was still totally optimistic about his condition. However, I had to educate myself and get a better picture of what this all meant.

May 31, 2019

That night, sleep was out of the question. As I sat in front of my computer in my home office, I began feverishly researching in order to get a better understanding of what was going on. I started with the functions of the liver and kidneys. I read about what exactly the difference was between heat exhaustion and other heat-related injuries. I researched the number of people on the organ transplant list yearly, daily. I read about the life expectancy of a liver transplant recipient and even about transplant recipients meeting the families of the donor.

There were two successful post-heat stroke transplant recipients performed at the University of Maryland. One was a young man by the name of Gavin Class who, like Jordan, was a football player who went down on the first day of practice. The other was a triathlete. They both had been treated at University of Maryland Shock Trauma with this new medical technology called an ECMO machine, just like Jordan.

ECMO, Extracorporeal Membrane Oxygenation, is a machine that helps provide support for patients with a sick heart, lungs, or in some cases, both. ECMO is used when traditional medical treatments have failed. ECMO does not treat the patient's disease it only supports the body while it tries to get better. This is what was keeping my beautiful, 19-year-old son alive.

I learned why it was so dire for Jordan to get liver support. The liver is the largest organ in the body, which produces proteins that are important with blood clotting. It is also one of the organs that breaks down old damaged blood cells. The liver plays a central role in all metabolic processes in the body. In fat metabolism, the liver cells can produce energy.

I learned why he needed support for his kidneys. The kidneys perform many crucial functions, including maintaining overall fluid balance, regulation and filtration of minerals from blood, waste filtration from food, medications and toxic substances.

I learned that people who have had a liver transplant have an 89% chance of survival after one year. The five-year survival rate is 75%.

I learned that as of 2018, almost 114,00 people in the United States were on the waiting list for a lifesaving organ transplant. Another name is added to the national transplant waiting list, on average, every 10 minutes.

I learned that 70% of people who undergo liver transplant live for at least 5 years. That means that for every

100 people who receive a liver transplant for any reason about 70 will live for 5 years and 30 will die in 5 years.

I also learned that there were 14,000 people waiting for a liver transplant in the United States. Thousands of people, who like my son, needed a new liver to live. The only problem was the median national waiting time was 321 days. I still didn't know what exactly was going on, but I knew that my son, sitting there in a coma, didn't have 321 days to wait.

My research that night also opened up the world of heat exhaustion—or what happens when your body simply gets too hot and your internal temperature reaches 104 degrees. The signs and symptoms of heat exhaustion include heavy sweating, muscle cramps and pale or cold skin.

Over time, heat exhaustion can lead to weakness or confusion, dark colored urine, dizziness and headache. Many people with ongoing heat exhaustion eventually experience nausea, vomiting and rapid heartbeat.

These are abnormalities that every young student athlete should be educated on. Signs and symptoms that they should know about in order to recognize a problem within their own bodies.

I also learned about heat stroke—a condition marked by fever and often by unconsciousness. It is an injury caused by the failure of the body's temperature regulating mechanism when exposed to excessively high temperatures. Heat stroke is much more serious than heat exhaustion. It can cause shock, organ failure, or brain damage in extreme cases. Heat stroke can kill you.

Heat stroke isn't one of those conditions that sneaks up on you or hides in plain sight, it's one that is marked by very specific, and noticeable signs and symptoms.

- Fever of 104°F or higher
- Flushed or red skin
- Lack of sweating even in heat
- Trouble breathing
- Fainting
- Seizures
- Loss of consciousness

These are fairly recognizable symptoms—something you would notice in a player or teammate. Something a trained athletic trainer should be able to notice in a stranger walking down the street.

To put it simply, when a person's body temperature goes above 104° F, it is the equivalent of their organs being placed in a microwave oven.

The longer your organs are in that microwave, the more your organs start to cook. The longer they are in the microwave, the more damage is done. You have a window of 15 to 20 minutes to cool your body temperature down to under 104° F before serious damage occurs. Jordan's core body temperature when he was finally was transported to the hospital was over 106°F—and he had been that way for over an hour and a half.

That night, I had a brutal crash course on what was going on with Jordan. Now I had a realistic idea of what happened. The heat stroke explained why he had a seizure at practice. It was starting to make some sense. How it actually happened would come later.

The Next Morning

We arrived at the hospital that morning, following a sleepless night of research and worry. We received updates from Doctor Scalea, the Head Physician at the Shock Trauma Center. It still hadn't dawned on Tonya and me how sick Jordan really was. He was still squeezing our fingers on command.

Jordan was intubated and strapped down to his hospital bed. He was hooked to every life support machine you can imagine. He needed machines for his heart, lungs, liver and kidney. Here was our son, who is so strong lying here, helpless. Our son, who is 300 pounds of muscle but still has enough baby fat on him to reveal his youth—and he can't even breathe on his own.

He was our big guy, our most prized possession, who fought so hard to be able to play football at this level, and now he was in this hospital bed fighting for his life. I knew at that moment; he was not going to play football again. But it was my job as a father to keep him motivated, inspired and uplifted to get through this. I had given Jordan so many "we're McNair's," pep talks and fatherly anecdotes throughout the years—but I needed more than that to motivate my son through this.

The meeting with doctors and specialist that afternoon started with discussions of a liver transplant. One of the specialists we talked to stated we would have a better pool of options if we'd consider a liver with Hepatitis C. My mind was still spinning from the evening before. I didn't know what implications came from taking a Hepatitis C liver. Clearly, I'd be spending another night in front of my computer again.

After another long day of prayer circles with family and friends, I was back in front of my computer. I researched what Hepatitis C, or Hep C, was and how it affected the liver. I was somewhat familiar with Hep C. I often see several of my clients diagnosed with this condition. However, I had no real knowledge of the disease, or what it would mean for my son.

Hepatitis C is a disease caused by a virus that infects the liver. A Hep C infection can lead to inflammation of the liver and can cause the immune system to attack healthy liver cells. It can spread through blood to blood contact. Most importantly, Hep C is treatable. And a liver with Hep C on a smiling Jordan seemed like a much better alternative than what I saw in front of me.

June 1st, 2018

We arrived at the hospital that morning and prepared for an 11:00 AM meeting with the transplant doctors. The conversation was quick.

"Mr. McNair, Ms. Wilson, Jordan is extremely sick. His liver is 85% necrotic and if you don't make a decision right now to do a liver transplant, he'll be dead within 12 hours."

There was a liver close by in Pennsylvania, a young man had just overdosed, and his liver was still healthy.

"Doctor, there's nothing else to discuss, get the liver please."

The transplant team prep started early that afternoon. As optimistic as we were as parents; how could we not continue to ask ourselves, "How did we get to this juncture?" How did a healthy kid Tuesday morning find himself preparing for liver transplant Friday evening? How can my Division 1 collegiate athlete find himself hours away from death if he doesn't have a life-saving organ transplant?

Jordan's liver transplant was performed at 9:30 PM on June 1, 2018. As we waited, the hospital staff in the ICU gave the family a Pink Book; a journal you write notes to your loved one in. You fill it with hopes and wishes that they will recover so that one day, they will be able to read all of the notes that you've written to them. This was significant in Jordan's recovery, as I was confident that he would read our notes to him in the book when he made it through this. We filled it with notes from his BFF Danae, Tonya and myself. It was therapeutic to all of us.

The hospital hallway to the ICU center had seemed to get longer and longer over the last few days. I couldn't make sense of it, why it was getting so long when I came in the hospital in the mornings. The stress and pressure of staying optimistic and strong for my family was getting to me. For the first time in my life, I felt totally impotent and powerless to help my son. My son, who I would instantly sacrifice my own life for, was facing the biggest challenge of his 19 years, and there was nothing I could do.

I often asked God why he took Jordan of all people. He was a young man who was 100 times better than me at 19 years old. He was everything I wasn't growing up. He didn't choose to become a statistic in Baltimore City's streets, he made all of the right choices. I thought that I could protect Jordan from all the mistakes I made. This was not only his most challenging battle but mine as well. I'd be dishonest if I didn't say I asked God to take me and spare his life.

I've lived 49 years, take me.

I spent Jordan's entire life trying to protect him from any pain the world could cause him. How could I protect him from what I didn't see or even know about?

How was I so trusting of these coaches who sat at our table before signing day promising to treat him as one of their own? These same coaches who didn't have the integrity to call us and tell us Jordan got hurt on the first day of conditioning drills. The same coach that didn't ride in the ambulance to the hospital with our son, after promising us that he'd protect him.

I made the wrong decision about who to trust with the thing that mattered most to me in the world.

Every time I walked into the hospital and towards my son's room to see the outcome of that decision, the hallway got longer. The walk was harder. The weight was more difficult to bear. I decided to trust another man to protect my son, my most prized possession, during the times I could not. And this is where that decision got us.

June 2nd, 2018

The first 24 hours after the transplant felt like an eternity. The transplant was a success overall. However, in the ICU, the term "success" meant Jordan's body hadn't reject the organ, at least so far. We still had an extremely long recovery road to recovery ahead of us.

My morning trips into the ICU were the most difficult part of my day. I would walk down that long hallway, my brain rampant with thoughts. The thought of Jordan fighting for his life was tearing me up inside. I felt like I had failed my son. It was impossible not to feel that way every time I walked down the hospital and toward my son strapped down to a hospital bed.

The walk down that hallway took so long, and I would completely lose it on my walk in every day. I was filled with anger, sadness—I was overcome with emotions I didn't even know I had. Then, I would get inside the elevator, take a deep breath and push it all to the back of my mind. I would force myself to put on an optimistic face for everyone else, and walk into the ICU a new, stoic, more composed version of myself. But inside, I was still screaming.

As I sat and waited for those first 24 hours, I took the opportunity to learn more about Gavin Class, the Towson State football player who had a similar heat-related injury as Jordan did. He had several surgeries after his liver transplant, and he fought his way through to a successful recovery. I was optimistic that Jordan would get through this too, just like Gavin. All of his life, I would tell him, "you're a McNair son, we don't die, we multiply." This was the one time, more than ever that I hoped I was right.

I had to keep myself focused mentally and physically to continue to motivate him during his road to recovery. However, I couldn't stop thinking about what happened that day at practice. I kept asking myself, if Tonya and I didn't know these things, how many other parents of student athletes don't know about these heat-related injuries?

June 3, 2018

It had been an extremely long weekend. The first 24 hours following a transplant are the most unpredictable. The day after the transplant, Jordan went into cardiac arrest. Tonya's cousin, Cori, who was a nurse at the hospital would check on Jordan during her shifts and keep us updated on his status.

When Jordan went into cardiac arrest she ran and grabbed Tonya immediately. She told Tonya to coach him back, that he needed to hear her. Tonya shouted with everything she had.

"Come on Jordan! You can do it!"

"You got this, Mommy is here."

"Come back to us!"

"Mommy is here."

And his heart started beating again. Just like that.

When they say a mother's love is powerful, these are the types of miracles they are talking about.

When a patient is that sick, you learn about a term called the ICU shuffle. It's one good shift, one bad shift, back and forth, and back again. It could be as big as cardiac arrest, or as simple as blood pressure failing to regulate without medication.

These were small hurdles in the big picture of Jordan's recovery, but that's what he was doing, shuffling back and forth.

That weekend, the hospital offered us a few classrooms to accommodate the hundreds of people that came to support us. Coaches, teammates, classmates, family members were all coming together to join Team Jordan. Family members were bringing their friends. Friends were bringing their families.

There were so many little children running around, it brought some much-needed joy to the situation. It's amazing what the children, so innocent and unaware of the tragedy around them, can do for your soul. Despite everything going on inside of that ICU room, I was truly in awe at all the love around us and all the support we received.

I spent that night in Jordan's hospital room. As difficult as it was to get some rest with the nonstop flow of nurses, I managed to briefly doze off before the next shift came on duty and those first 24 hours came to a close.

Pink Book Entry
Monday 6/4/18

Jordan,

I know this event has changed all of our lives very quickly. We went from you waking up a healthy guy Tuesday morning 5/29/2018 to a liver transplant Friday 6/1/2018.

As a family we are rolling with punches and adapting to whatever changes God has in store for us. This is a clear indicator that obviously the plan can change, usually for the better, at any time. I'm confident you'll touch a lot more people when this ordeal is over.

Jordan, I don't know if you heard all of your visitor's voices who've come to see you with their love, support, and encouragement for you to keep fighting. The love for you has been overwhelming. Ace, you now have a mission to make a difference once you get through this.

Keep fighting, as I've always told you "You're a McNair we don't die we multiply."

Love,
Dad

June 4th, 2018

I awoke to one of the nurses telling me that her supervisor needed to talk to me in private. After listening to the morning report from Jordan's nurses and doctors, I went to meet with the Nursing Supervisor.

"Mr. McNair, with all the attention and support that Jordan is receiving from everyone, clearly there is something significant going on here. There are too many people from the coaching staff prodding in Jordan's charts. We don't go to UMD interfering with the work that they do. You should consider limiting visitors to immediate family only as Jordan is extremely sick."

I was thinking the coaches and supporters from the football team were genuine. Some were. But some were clearly trying to cover something up. I didn't know it at the time, but they were trying to mask the fatal mistakes that put us all here. I texted DJ Durkin and informed him that all visitation from anyone other than immediate family had come to a halt, and that I would keep him updated on Jordan's progress.

From the moment Tonya and I walked into that emergency room at Washington Adventist Hospital, we felt a disingenuous energy from certain members of the coaching staff. Someone had made a serious blunder that day on the field regarding Jordan's injury. We would find out sooner rather than later what really happened to our son.

Up until this point, Tonya and I had been through a crash course in medical terminology and conditions, but we were still trying to keep up. I often found myself saying to nurses, "I wasn't in your nursing school class, could you explain this to me as if I was a 5-year-old?"

This seemed to help me understand a lot more about what was going on with Jordan. We were spending between 12-18 hours each day at the Shock Trauma Center. When you are that tired and that drained, anything that makes processing information easier is a welcome reprieve.

That day, I learned that Jordan's lactic acid levels were extremely high. When the oxygen level is low, carbohydrates are broken down for energy and it makes lactic acid. Lactic acid levels get higher during strenuous exercise. They also spike when you have other conditions such as heart failure, severe infections, sepsis, or shock that lowers the flow of blood and oxygen throughout the body.

I was also introduced to the term lactic acidosis. Lactic acidosis is a form of metabolic acidosis that begins when a person over produces or underutilizes lactic acid, and their body isn't able to adjust to the accompanying changes. People with lactic acidosis have problems with their liver, and sometimes their kidneys, being able to remove excess acid from their body.

When Jordan went into liver failure before his transplant, his body started to fail, *quickly*. His 300-pound frame simply wasn't able to recover, as all of his organs began shutting down at once.

That hallway to ICU was getting longer and longer those days. It was taking even more time for me to make my way down the corridor. The weight of my failures kept that walk as slow and as difficult as ever. I kept telling myself the better he got, the shorter the hallway would get and the easier the journey would seem. But it never did.

Pink Book Entry
Tuesday 6/5/2018

Hey Big Fella,

I left the hospital around 2:30 AM. It's impossible to get any rest while the nurses are in there working with you. Your vitals and other stuff are consistent right now.

12:08pm

Ace, just spoke with your transplant doctors they said, "The other part of your surgery was a success." They sewed you up and put a mesh screen in your abdomen.

Don't worry you'll be doing crunches in no time. I'm committed to staying in just as good shape as you, even though I have a head start.

I love you Ace,
Dad

June 5th - 10th

The entire week was a blur. Most of our time was spent meeting with doctors and nurses. We also had to go down to Maryland to clean out Jordan's dorm, a seemingly trivial task given what we were dealing with at home.

Within a few days of Jordan's accident, the media had started sniffing out the story, and soon, Jordan's fight was all over the news. Perhaps they suspected foul play at the time, perhaps it was the hundreds of people gathered at the hospital to support him, or perhaps it was just the startling concept of a healthy Division 1 athlete ending up in a coma.

I now not only had to live this nightmare every day but hear about it on the news as well.

There was a lot of hope and prayer circles surrounding us, and so many prayer warriors who were dedicated Jordan's recovery. As a faith-based family, we had no shortage of prayer warriors on our side. We were confident that Jordan would pull through this with God's guidance. Who knew his 19 years may have had a different purpose than we thought after all?

We did have one other highlight that week, a visit from the Class family. Gavin Class, the Towson State football player who had a liver transplant following a heatstroke, and his wonderful mom, Danielle came to see us. Even with how bad things were looking for us, it was the shot of hope that we needed.

Pink Book Entry
Wednesday 6/6/2018

Ace,

Danae spent the night with you last night. She's been a loyal BFF through this process.

Your story has been all over the news. Ace this has been an extremely difficult process for us all. When you read this, you'll be amazed at the competitive fighter you are as I've always told you were all of your life.

Gavin Class was a Towson State football player who like you suffered a heat stroke in 2013 or 2014. I'm sure Gavin and his mom Danielle will play a major part in your recovery process. They are the new members of our family.

Their visit was very inspirational yesterday. Meeting Gavin gave us the confidence you'll make it through too.

Love,
Dad

Gavin's Story

Gavin Class is a great young man who, like Jordan, was a collegiate offensive lineman. He attended Towson State University, located just north of Baltimore City. While at practice on August 12, 2013, Gavin suffered an exertional heat stroke on the last sprint of the day during a two-a-day practice.

His body had reached an estimated 111°F on the field. Upon arrival to the hospital, Gavin was in a coma with significant organ failure. The emergency room doctors told his family that he would "probably not make it through the night." But he did.

Gavin was also transported to the Shock Trauma Center where his heart stopped, and he needed to be resuscitated. The doctors again told his family that Gavin was as close to dying without being dead. After he was stabilized, it was determined that Gavin needed a liver transplant.

Gavin's life was saved by the incredible staff at the University of Maryland Medical Center, and of course, by an organ donor. When the surgery was done, Gavin had to relearn how to walk, talk, and preform the basic functions that we all take for granted on a daily basis.

During some intense rehabilitation, deep spirituality, loving parents, and an even tougher father who challenged him during his entire rehabilitation, he made it back.

Meeting Gavin and Danielle was the motivation we needed to keep fighting for Jordan and to get prepared for his rehab when the time came. I just knew that no matter how this fight for his life looked at this time, it was a journey we were going to be on to get Jordan back to being Jordan.

The difference between our two stories was the day Gavin was injured there was a cold-water tub on the field. His coached recognized the signs and symptoms of an exertional heat-related injury right away. They knew to put Gavin in the tub to get his core body temperature down then proceeded to call 911. It's the cool first, transport second model.

After the EMT's arrived they made the critical mistake of taking Gavin out of the cold-water tub too early and without out taking his temperature. They did not know this critical step at the time, it is the EMT's protocol to get someone to a hospital as quickly as possible. They should have left Gavin in the tub until his body temp was down to at least 104°F before transporting him. Following this protocol would have meant no organ failure, no liver transplant and no near-death experience. In fact, more likely than not, Gavin would have returned to the team the next day.

Instead of getting back to football, Gavin's injury led to over 15 surgeries, cancer, and he was never able to play the game he loved again.

The difference in these stories is that on May 29, 2018 there was no cold-water tub on the practice field. While Jordan was visibly having a heat stroke, the athletic trainers ignored the signs and symptoms of his exertional heat injury. Instead of getting him the type of help Gavin got, when Jordan started showing the signs of heat stroke, his head athletic trainer responded to his cries for help by yelling, "Drag his ass across the field. If he can't walk, drag his ass."

Pink Book Entry
Thursday 6/7/2018

Ace,

Mom and I went down to get your clothes out of your junky room. I had to prepare her for what she might find in your personal belongings. I now know you got your love for sneakers honestly from me. Funny while walking down the hallway to your apartment I remember my college dorm years.

We stayed in dorms with community bathrooms. Oh yeah, like the ones you stayed in during football training camp last summer. You're fighting today, this road to recovery is a dance two steps forward, one step back. Today as well as yesterday has been a one step back day.

Blood bacteria infections as well as your blood pressure getting to a normal level on its own. Kyle Locke, Noah's dad is here with us today he works in the hospital. The Locke's have been extremely supportive as well as a lot of other people.

Keep fighting,
Dad

Getting to the Truth

Those two weeks in the hospital were so surreal, at times it almost felt like it was happening to someone else. I was exhausted and spent every waking hour I could trying to educate myself on what was medically happening to my son. Then there was the liver transplant, the hundreds of supporters, and now the added media coverage. However, even with all of this going on, we were really just trying to focus on the only thing that mattered—saving Jordan's life.

I couldn't see it at the time, but that influx of coaches and athletic trainers the first few days was intentional. They were attempting to bombard us with information that took the focus off of them and put *their* side of the story in the forefront of our minds. I remember the one team doctor initially told us Jordan had everything *except* heat stroke, even though at that point in my journey of self-education, I was confident that a heat-related injury was to blame.

I've never been one to not recognize deception when I feel or see it. I have been through too much and met too many of the wrong people to not be able to see right through it. Yet, in the moment, my radar was off and I didn't make the initial realization that I was being duped by these men.

Tonya and I wanted to know what happened that day, however our entire focus was on Jordan and on keeping him alive. Things were moving so fast. Tonya and I were still trying to figure out what happened from Tuesday until Friday. When the nurse had a serious talk with us about the school's coaches and athletic department sniffing around Jordan's charts, I slowly began to wonder if there was more to the story than what I was being told.

Then Tonya and I began to hear whispers of stories about that day. I think some people were trying to protect us from the details, but we started to suspect we may not know the whole story. Our plan was to get to the bottom of it when the time was right. At the time, nothing else mattered besides Jordan's recovery.

As the crowds of supporters and friends continued to gather in the hospital, there was a strong group of our McDonogh School family there by our side. I always loved the tight-knit community at that school. The football coaches played a significant part in Jordan's athletic development and he and his teammates always stayed connected to their coaches, even when they went off to college.

There was a family-like loyalty and a bond in that McDonogh community and I trusted them in their support of Jordan during this uncertain time.

One day, one of my fellow McDonogh family members pulled me aside in the midst of all this and told me, "What they're telling you is bullshit, that's not what happened to Jordan." He then sent me a copy of an emotional text message from one of Jordan's McDonogh teammates who was on the field with Jordan when he was injured.

In his text message, he was understandably shaken, as any 20-year-old would be, at how the athletic training staff ignored Jordan's pleas for help. How the head athletic trainer yelled, "If he can't walk, drag his ass across the field."

This kid was clearly blown away by how they could do this to one of his teammates and friends. A lot of young people at this age still have a sense of purity to them. They don't lie, especially when they see an injustice being done to someone they care about.

I was very strategic at that time about what information I shared with Tonya. She was trying her best to stay strong and optimistic, as any mother would be, with her only son fighting for his life. These people who did this to Jordan were still visiting him in the hospital, so I didn't want to add any more emotional strain to what she was dealing with already. So, I began my own fact-finding mission.

I was trying to be an example of strength for Tonya and the rest of the family and put on a stoic face while I attempted to get to the truth.

At that moment, I was confident I could deal with the information of what really happened that day better than anyone else in the family. But what I discovered was far worse than what I imagined.

Pink Book Entry
Friday 6/09/2018

Ace,

told myself the hallway in the hospital to the Shock Trauma Unit is
going to look shorter from now on.

The shorter it gets the stronger you'll get. Ace, Danae has been
walking a little dog name Hank I keep telling her to sneak him in
your room as a therapy dog lol.

You're getting better Champ keep fighting.

Love,
Dad

What Really Happened
May 29th, 2018

We knew Jordan was going to his first day of practice as an incoming sophomore on May 29th, 2018. And we knew the first day of practice is the day most football players dread. For the University of Maryland, this first day of practice means two conditioning drills, Gassers and 110s.

Gassers get their name for a reason and are often touted as the toughest sprint drill for football players at any level. Players run in position groups and sprint from sideline to sideline four times. Other variances have players run to the sideline and back, and then each hash-mark and back.

Then, there were the 110s, a conditioning drill that has you start on the edge of the field and sprint 110 yards in the time designated by your position. If you are an offensive lineman, you are expected to cover 110 yards in 21 seconds with one minute and fifteen seconds rest between each sprint. Once you cross the goal line your allotted rest begins. Then you repeat. And repeat, and repeat.

According to a report that came out after Jordan's accident, the team began running these drills at 4:15 PM. According to players, they had been conditioning for approximately 45 minutes when Jordan became overheated between his fifth and seventh sprint. He went from sprinting to a slow jog. On his last return sprint, he had slowed down even more, was visibly in distress and couldn't complete his run. His teammates had to go help him; Jordan could barely stand.

They then helped him over to the athletic trainer, the same athletic trainer that told them to "drag hiss ass off the field," if he couldn't run. Jordan was in visible distress displaying all the signs and symptoms of a heat-related injury. *Confusion, irritability, dizziness and vomiting.*

The athletic training staff kept him on the field because they wanted him to practice more. That is what they felt was more important than a 19-year-old boy being unable to breathe or stand. They walked him up the entire length of the football field instead of getting him to a cold-water tub, not that there was even one on the field to begin with. At the time, Jordan's body temperature was above 104°F and he was having a full heat stroke. It is estimated that this happened around 5 PM. Then, the most difficult part of the story came.

When Jordan was on the field, confused and irritable, he began crying out for his mother. "Call my mother," he was saying. "Call my mother." Jordan was in the middle of a heat stroke, agitated, not able to think straight, but still begging for help. Still fighting. He was swearing on anyone, even my own mother's life, that something was wrong, and he was in distress. I know my son, there is hardly anything in the world that would cause him to say something like it.

Here was a 6'5, 300-pound Division 1 football player, pleading for his mother. And nobody helped him. The thought of that sends chills down my body every time I think about that. To think that my son spent those last conscious moments on the field, pleading for help, while a bunch of grown men, fathers, with children of their own just ignored him. It still makes me sick to this day.

While Jordan was laying there, begging for help, his body was in a microwave. His organs were cooking. The 15-30-minute time frame of getting his temperature down in a cold-water tub had passed and his body temperature continued to rise.

Then Jordan started seizing, which is one of the most notable signs of a serious heat stroke. His body temperature rose above 108°F and that's where it stayed for nearly an hour. When reports about Jordan's accident started circulating around the press, it would be referred to as an "unexplained hour." Unexplained. No one could explain to us what they were doing during that hour as my son sat there begging for his mother.

Finally, at 5:58 PM a campus police officer called 9-1-1. Not an athletic trainer, not a strength and conditioning coach and not a member of the coaching staff—a campus police officer. It was 6:36 PM before Jordan reached the hospital that night.

When he arrived at the hospital nearly 90 minutes after his original heat stroke symptoms, his body temp was still over 108°F. Jordan's organs were in that microwave oven process for an excessive amount of time, and they got there from a heat-related injury that is entirely preventable. With a realistic emergency action plan, Jordan could have been saved, just like many student athletes today can be saved. It isn't all that difficult and it doesn't require a great deal of medical knowledge. It's a plan that any athletic trainer should be able to implement in case something like this happens.

Now we saw why Jordan was so sick by the time he got to the hospital. Now we see why he had a seizure. Now we saw why his liver was 85% dead by the 31st of May. Jordan's body was dying internally the entire time they kept him on the field and every minute they failed to get him help, his body died even more. Now looking back at those days in the hospital, Superman couldn't have survived that one.

Pink Book Entry
Saturday 6/10/2018

Ace,

Today is Saturday I started the day off by playing golf at 7:20 am. It was Coach Bub's first time playing and he looked pretty good. I'm still advocating for him to invest in some lessons. Grandma Susie is in the hospital probably worried about you as we all are. She's doing fine they were just running some test on her so don't you worry any.

Ace you had a very interesting visitor from a friend of a friend of mine. Her name is Jael she asked if she could visit with you. She has a very strong spiritual connection to a higher power. She asked your name before introducing herself to you. She stated she only felt life in this room especially from you and it's not your time to go anywhere but to a higher level.

She also stated among may things that you weren't feeling well prior to practice Tuesday maybe three days before you had some flu like symptoms coming on. That's the second time we heard that from someone spiritually connected. Karen's friend Prophet said the exact same thing. One thing she felt from you that you weren't a talker and a you are a man of a few words. She also mentioned you are a wise man. Boy I taught you well!

Ace you had quite a few visitors yesterday. The Coaches from Hamilton have been consistently coming to see you. Coach Mike, Coach Kevin, and another big guy I don't recall his name. I'm saving the PJ's visit for last, he came home for graduation and wanted to see you before he went back to Penn State for summer practice. Your pup kept calling you Big Dog.

Ok Big Dog keep fighting.

Love,

Dad

June 11, 2018

By June 11th, we were still doing the ICU shuffle, continuing this figurative dance between hope and despair. You can have two good days, but never two bad days. On June 11th Jordan had his second bad day. The life support machines were literally doing everything for him.

We sincerely thought that the liver transplant was what he needed to recover. A liver transplant isn't like installing a new battery into a radio that doesn't work anymore, even if you optimistically think that it will. A one-motor boat couldn't raise the Titanic after most of it already sank in the ocean. One liver transplant wasn't going to bring my son back after everything his body went through.

Too much time had elapsed before Jordan got help. Too much damage had been done. He was dying internally while on the field that day, calling for his mother. My son put up a hell of a fight while in the hospital those two weeks. I couldn't have been prouder about how hard he fought to stay with us—but his body had sustained too much damage. And even a 300-pound body as big and as strong as his couldn't come back from it.

By the next morning, the loss of oxygen to Jordan's brain and the impact of two bad days in a row meant things weren't looking good. That night, when we all left the hospital, that hallway from the ICU seemed shorter for some reason. Finally, after so many days, it stopped getting longer and my walk stopped getting heavier. Tonya and I were in a calm space. We left the hospital with a strong feeling of peace and acceptance.

Our immediate family members and close friends who were at the hospital that evening with us all walked up the street from the hospital for a bite to eat. While eating, we all laughed, smiled and shared our memorable stories and experiences with Jordan.

Jordan was blessed to have a loving family who all shared in his accomplishments and successes. The love and support that Tonya and I had while raising him was extremely helpful not only in those last two weeks, but throughout his entire life. His relationships with every single one of these family members was unique in its own way.

They always say it takes a village to raise a child. While Tonya and I put in so much of ourselves to raise our son, it was Team Jordan that still made it all possible. Like the time we had to pass the hat around so I could take Jordan to the Army Combine in San Antonio. It was an opportunity for Jordan to compete with the nation's top underclassmen in front of top college football scouts. His village believed in him and knew chipping in would help get him to the next level.

There were so many times this village showed up like this. I had always been an entrepreneur, so money was tight more than once for me. Our village always invested collectively in all our family members. It was amazing. Jordan's "Nana" would drive 30 minutes to take him to school 15 minutes away. His "Pop" would pick him up and give him driving lessons before I bought him his first car. He never hesitated to give Grandma Suzy a ride anywhere she needed to go. He always seemed to pick his cousins up from their basketball practices or take friends to their conditioning training.

He wasn't just a recipient of the goodwill of this village, he was a central part of it.

Pink Book Entry
Monday 6/12/2018

We decided to stop making entries in Jordan's pink book.

June 13, 2018
An Angel Is Called Home

My phone rang that morning at 5:30 AM.

"Mr. McNair, this is Doctor Green you should come to the hospital. We don't expect Jordan to make it through the day. He has lost oxygen to his brain; his brain is dead."

I think Tonya and I both felt it that night when we left the hospital. As much as we prayed, our village of family, friends and supporters prayed it was time to let God take Jordan home. Jordan, armed with all of the love, support, and everything else positive we could pour into him as parents, fought his best fight.

On June 13, 2018 at 11:00 AM, we said goodbye to our wonderful human being. A son, grandson, nephew, teammate, BFF, Bro and thought leader who never gave Tonya and I, or our village an ounce of trouble. Who just wanted to work hard and fulfil his dream of playing football. Who he left our world surrounded by love, which, when your time comes, is all you can really ask for.

As our village surrounded Jordan's hospital bed with tears of grief and sadness, we all said our final goodbyes, we all knew that he was in a better place at that time. His fight was over, and God had him.

JORDAN MARTIN McNAIR

Jordan and his parents at his 16th birthday party.

Senior Night at McDonogh High School.

Jordan with a fan after winning the Price Memorial Trophy.

Jordan's official visit to Ohio State.

18th birthday trip to Universal Studios. Jordan's last trip with his father.

Jordan as a University of Maryland Terrapin.

Jordan's teammate Ellis McKennie III waving the #79
flag honoring Jordan.

Our first time speaking nationally on Good Morning
America with Michael Strahan.

The first ever Jordan McNair Health and Wellness Sports Clinic.

Tonya and Martin testifying before a senate committee for House Bill 876, The Jordan McNair Act.

PART IV

June 20th, 2018
Jordan's Home Going Service

For some reason, I wore all white for my son's viewing service. I don't remember the exact reason I put it on that day, but more likely than not, I knew that not all of the energy I would face that day would be pure. When Jordan died, my main focus was to send him off as peacefully as we could, and now it was time for the rest of his friends, family and teammates to send him off as well.

I knew there would be members of Jordan's coaching staff there that day. The chess game I had been playing, of not showing emotion towards the coaching staff was extremely challenging, especially at times like this. I knew at this point that they had caused this—they were the reason we were all here. It's an indescribable feeling to have to look at the faces of the men who literally killed your child and to not act violently or negatively towards them. It's even worse when you have to look at them the day you bury your son.

We experienced immeasurable agony over losing our only son, yet we found a certain peace knowing this battle was over. It was devastating because we lost a son who had so much life to live, yet peaceful because we knew that he was in a better place.

Leading up until that day, my good friend, and the current University of Maryland head football coach, Michael Locksley would call me every day. Michael had been calling me regularly with a prayer or words of support. He and his wife, Kia, had lost their son Meiko to a senseless murder in September of 2017. If anyone understood and could feel my pain as a father losing a son, Mike could.

The morning of the funeral Mike asked how I was doing. I told him I was OK, but ready to get it over with. Jordan's death was the first death I'd ever experienced in my immediate family. Both of my parents were still living, and I didn't know what to expect. He let me know that the viewing would seem like a blur. He also told me "I know you think that you're strong for your family, however, stand close to someone you trust when they close the casket."

Mike was right, it was a blur. Thousands of people came to pay their respects. While I was moved to see how many lives my son had touched, the entire experience was such a haze. It was so difficult to keep it together and to not only keep my grief from swallowing me up, but my anger.

Then I saw Maryland's head athletic trainer. All I could hear in my mind was him yelling, "drag his ass across the field." When it was his turn in line for the viewing, my blood began to boil. The emotional pressure was killing me on the inside. We still hadn't done a full investigation on what happened, I was too preoccupied with funeral arrangements and burial plots—but I did know some things. I knew there was at least one person who should have acted with moral and ethical integrity as a medical professional, but who failed to do so. And one of these men was in the funeral home where I was holding a celebration for my son.

Tonya and I were standing near Jordan's casket greeting the long line of supporters when I saw him walking down the aisle towards us. Then, for the first time since this all started, my emotions finally got the best of me. I grabbed him, put my arm around his shoulder and slowly whispered some choice words into his ear. I encouraged him to distance himself, miles away from me. If he ever saw me again, our conversation would be ending much differently than it did that day.

After he left, I knew I still had to keep my composure and speak to the thousands of supporters of family, friends, parents, teammates, classmates and coaches that were there that day. I found it therapeutic to share experiences from Jordan's life. Like when he had to take his driver's test multiple times. He was so nervous that last attempt. I was already ready to give him the Michael Jordan speech. To remind him that Michael Jordan went to the NBA Eastern Conference finals three times against the Detroit Pistons before the Chicago Bulls won their first championship. But Jordan emerged with that huge gap-toothed smile that day at the MVA, so excited about his latest victory. So, I gladly pocketed my MJ speech away for another time.

I talked of our many college visits when I was a struggling business owner and unsure of how to figure out the finances behind taking him. The countless father and son stories and memories of those Sundays together.

I told a lot of stories, our stories. And they garnered quite a few smiles and laughs on that somber day. Every parent in attendance understand that these stories of love and sacrifice were all in an attempt to give my son a better life than I had, to help him be better than me.

Finally, when the day came to an end, and they closed the casket on my precious son—I completely broke down in tears, just like Mike said I would.

Five Days Later
June 25, 2018

On June 25th, 2018, Dr. Rod Walters was hired by the University of Maryland to do an investigation into Jordan's death. He was called for the report on the day Jordan died. At this point, the media coverage surrounding Jordan had escalated and people from all over the country were asking how a young, college athlete could just die during practice.

Dr. Walters is a sports medicine consultant and the first professional hired to investigate what happened the day Jordan was injured. We initially felt we would be voiceless against a big institution like the University of Maryland.

He was a consultant of the school's choice and we felt there was no way the report wouldn't go in their favor. We had an initial gut feeling that whoever was writing the check would be determining what would eventually go in this final report. Tonya and I had never heard of this consultant. We never had a reason to know who he was or what he did.

We initially thought that this investigation would be biased. I personally thought the whole thing was a giant dog and pony show. The school had already put their own twist on the story when they spoke to the media, and I thought the "external investigation" was just another formality they could add to the headline.

I later found that Dr. Walters was as straight as an arrow. He called it like he saw it, right or wrong. Dr. Walters came in and began probing around to find out what really happened. He wanted to know what safety plan was, and most importantly, was not implemented that day.

At this point, we still hadn't spoken to the media, we had stayed silent. We were suppressing a lot of feelings and emotions about what we had been hearing, about how the players, our sons were being intimidated within this football program. The world had only heard the University of Maryland's side of things, while we were starting to learn more and more about what really went on behind closed doors.

I heard the investigator gave everyone an opportunity to share their memory of the events that day Jordan was injured. All of the players who wanted to speak to him had to sign their name on a sign-up sheet. The signup sheet was posted directly on the Director of Operation's office door.

In order to speak with the investigator, players had to do interviews in the coach's conference room, across from DJ Durkin's office. This is the same head coach who implemented this horrific environment of bullying and intimidation and who threatened to take students' scholarships away. And students had to sit in a conference room across from his office in order to participate in an investigation against him.

Obviously, the investigator didn't know this, because if he did, I'm sure he would have gone with a more anonymous approach. I'm sure there were players who wanted to sign the list and speak up, but didn't believe that they felt safe or protected by the people who were intimidating them the most, their coaches.

I'm not saying that all of the coaches on the team were to blame. When you're at the mercy of leadership, all you can do is hope nothing bad happens on your watch. I never realized why a handful of coaches only stayed one season and left so quickly. They were brave enough to get away from that environment as soon as they could.

Intimidation factors aside, there were five young men willing to step up. I love and respect these brave and honorable teammates who had the courage and strength to step forward and tell us what really happened that day. Two of these young men were Jordan's McDonogh brothers. When I finally got to listen to their stories, I noticed they all started by asking if their names would be mentioned in the report. I suppose that should have prepared me for what I was about to hear.

Their stories all had the same undertone. They talked of intimidation, emasculation, bullying and threats. These kids were sincerely worried that their scholarships would be taken away. These were big, strong, Division 1 football players, and you could hear the fear in their stories, because underneath their giant exterior, they were just young boys getting their first real taste of the injustices of the world.

One of these young men was just happy to be free from the bullying. He was graduating the following year and he didn't want to get on these coaches' radars again. He said once you got on their bad sides, they would make life miserable for you.

I also heard stories of one particular punishment, a workout area called the Pit. If you were injured or a problematic player, you were made to work out in the Pit. No one wanted to go to the Pit. In the Pit, you worked out over a bed of rocks. You were coached by a member of the strength and conditioning staff to lift weights, push the sled, do pushups or sit-ups until you passed out. That was the goal.

This was an opportunity to make an example out of anyone who was injured. Injuries were a bad thing—and you needed to learn to practice and play through it. Instead of sending injured players inside for rehabilitation or to work with a medical professional—you went to the Pit.

These stores made me think about when Jordan tore his pectoral muscle. Apparently, one of these guys begged him to get it checked out. But Jordan was likely too scared to say that he was injured, because he feared the Pit and any other repercussions that would come from being "weak" and sitting out. Hearing these stories made me understand why Jordan handled the injury the way he did.

As I was hearing all of these stories, I couldn't stop thinking about what we unknowingly sent Jordan into. This isn't what the coaches who sat at our kitchen were selling.

These teammates who were older played under a previous head coach. They knew the difference between what hard work looked like and what intimidation and bullying did. Jordan's class didn't have the measuring stick that his older teammates had. Even if we had probed Jordan to see how things were really going, he probably thought that this was the norm. He probably thought that bullying, fat shaming, and emasculating you was part of the college football experience.

Football is sold as a gateway to a better life for many of these kids. They see successful, confident men sitting at their kitchen tables promising them the world, giving them doctored Sports Illustrated covers and showing them their potential NFL salaries. Football is supposed to be a ticket to something better, protection from what kids like me often fall into. These kids came to Maryland to play football based off a dream they were sold—only to walk into a systemic nightmare.

The stories I heard were horrendous and difficult to listen to. The young men who stood up wanted this toxic behavior to stop. They knew it was wrong. But who would they tell this to? Or much less, who would believe them? They all agreed that it wasn't a matter of how but when someone would get seriously hurt. And that someone was Jordan.

No parent sends their student athlete away to be bullied, threatened, intimated or abused in any form. We send our children away to higher educational institutions to be developed mentally, physically, and emotionally. We want them to become better adults, to learn from their teachers and coaches so they can be better prepared to deal with life.

These boys didn't have strong role models like this to help mold them into successful adults. They had role models that would throw small weights and objects towards players who made them mad. They had examples of men who would force players to overeat to the point of vomiting. They had a head strength and conditioning coach with a mantra of "You're going to run so hard today, you'll see Jesus." Unfortunately, in Jordan's case, that mantra became his reality.

The Loss and The Grief

Losing Jordan at 19 years old brought about a type of devastation I didn't know I could experience, yet it had a profound impact on my life. I have always believed in staying in the present, especially after everything I've been through. It was one of the things that allowed me to accept that Tonya and I had a beautiful, wonderful gift of a son for 19 years, even though I wanted him around much longer.

Neither of us had any regrets on how we co-parented or raised Jordan. Those last two weeks in the hospital while Jordan was fighting for his life were the most challenging time in his life, as well as ours. And while it was completely gut wrenching to lose him, I couldn't help but think of how blessed I was to have such a wonderful human being for a son as long as I did.

Losing a child is not natural. It is not the order that life should go. However, it's a reality that happens far too often. Our grief was beyond words. Every emotion we felt was so extreme. How could it not be? As a parent, you try to do everything you can to protect your child, to take all of the hurt and pain away from them. And when they die, you want to blame yourself. We felt we put him in an unsafe environment. We trusted someone who we really didn't know, and the outcome of that decision was far worse than we ever could have predicted.

I think back to when Jordan was just a baby and how scared I was to let him go to daycare—to let someone else watch over him and care for him. I think about how worried I was, and how I would show up unannounced to check in on him and make sure he was OK. I didn't know I would need those same protective instincts when Jordan was a 300-pound adult.

Tonya and I think about these coaches often, and about how they were while sitting at our kitchen table recruiting Jordan. We go through it over and over again. We wonder, "Did we ask the right questions? What questions didn't we ask?"

You question God. You wonder "why my child?" He was a good kid, who had the whole world in front of him. He was as good as they come.

When your child dies, part of you dies with them. You lose an entire piece of yourself. No parent should ever feel the anguish and despair that comes with that. It's just not natural. The loss is something you never get used to. I know a mother's love is different from a father's love, but it's an empty space in your heart and soul just the same. My grief as a father looks different than Tonya's.

The loss of a child and the blame you can place on yourself can do one of two things: it can negatively consume you, or it can motivate you to do something. It can empower you to want to make sure no other parent ever feels this loss. Tonya and I chose option number two.

I would be lying to say that I didn't need therapy and grief counseling, especially with all of the media attention to come. Jordan's story was one of the most highlighted sports stories in 2018. Imagine reliving the worst thing to ever happen to you, every day when you see your child's photo on the news. The mental and emotional feelings tied to Jordan's death were beyond words. The media attention was overwhelming. And the university's version of events were not consistent with what really happened.

The story of the Pit wasn't the end of it. There were countless stories painting a picture of a horrific environment. One where players were bullied, called names, fat shamed, intimidated, not by other players, but by the same coaches that sat at our table that day. I was angry, resentful, confused, frustrated and blindsided to say the least.

A reporter by the name of Heather Dinich at ESPN wrote an article exposing the Maryland football program, and suddenly the word "toxic culture," seemed to be everywhere. Heather was adamant that there was foul play, and persistent in her efforts to unveil what was really going on. Her article detailed even more stories of foul, vulgar and humiliating tactics that put the well-being of *all* of these kids at risk.

She had more stories and insights about the University of Maryland football program than even I knew of. Heather's story painted a picture of what a toxic sports environment could really look like. Even as someone who knew this culture existed, I was still enraged by the details I read in her article. It was so difficult reading about this head coach who we felt so loyal to during Jordan's recruitment—acting like a monster. I have met so many people through the years; prisoners, addicts, criminals, people who society labels as "bad" yet I wasn't able to see the true corruption in front of me. How did I miss that? I still take full responsibility for it to this day.

Don't get me wrong I know that football has always been a gladiator sport with a rough mentality. I was also aware that most college football programs would break a player down mentally and physically to develop them into an elite competitor, but this was beyond comprehension. In fact, I always liked to see the pictures of the physical development of a player 12 -18 months after they started consistently working in the weight room with the right diet.

That was also motivation for most players during their recruitment process, to see what hard work at the collegiate level can do.

When you're looking at schools, the skill set of the strength and conditioning coaches that help foster these physical transformations among young people was just as appealing as all the bling. I had no idea about the tactics truly involved with getting these results. I'm sure that many college football programs used the same approach, the same type of the language and emasculation to motivate student athletes to push pass their limits. However, this group of men took it way too far and had to put their own demented twist on the process.

Any parent wants to react when someone has hurt their child, it is human nature. But the feelings you have when someone causes their death are unlike any you could imagine.

An entire system failed our son. A system that allowed a 40-year-old grown adult to create a toxic environment of intimidation and abuse of young men. These young men were there to learn, to grow, and to live out their dream of playing football. That is why they went to college.

The entire time Jordan was fighting for his life, this same coach, didn't have the integrity to apologize for not protecting him. It was emotionally draining not to beat the brakes off of this guy every time I saw him. A few days after Jordan passed, this coach and his wife came to Tonya's house to bring some food and refreshments. Three of my friends had to talk me out of not grabbing him by his throat that day. It was so hard to keep my composure while this man stood there with this smug look on his face. He knew he failed Jordan. He didn't know how to be a man and admit it. And his face said it all.

Tonya and I both had to literally suppress all of those feelings because our legal team didn't want us to make any comments publicly until we got the full story of what happened. I spoke to the mother of Marquese Meadow, a young student athlete who died on August 24, 2014 as a result of complications of a heat stroke. He was running in a punishment practice drill during football practice at Morgan State University. She told me, "I felt as though I didn't have a voice." Her words rang in my ears.

How many other parents felt this way who've lost their sons or daughters to this type of injury? I couldn't let my emotions get the best of me. I couldn't lash out and let my actions speak louder than my words. I needed to keep my composure; for myself, for Jordan, for Tonya and for other parents who felt they didn't have a voice either.

Something Must Be Done

We were told early on that Jordan had a heat-related injury. We had no idea what a heat stroke was, nor did we know how fatal it would be.

Our grief, pain and passion fueled the fire to start The Jordan McNair Foundation on June 16, 2018, three days after Jordan passed. The learning experience of what we just endured over those last two weeks was life shattering. There were so many statistics we didn't know at the time. We also didn't know how many of the other student athletes that had died as a result of an exertional heat injury.

Jordan was a lifelong athlete since he was five years old. He played every sport the average kid plays like flag football, baseball and basketball. And all of these sports required a yearly physical.

We assumed that a physical was all we needed to worry about to make sure it was safe for our child to play. We, like thousands of other parents, also just assumed the coaches knew what they were doing. You assume it at the AAU level, high school level, and without a doubt at the college level. We, as parents, get conditioned along the way with the mentality of "coaches coach and parents parent."

In other words, "Mom and Dad, I'm the subject matter expert here you're not so stay out of my way." The higher the level, the quieter the parents get towards coaches. And the more coaches start to ignore us.

The average parents of a student athlete only really ever asked two questions. One, "Can my child play?" And two, "How much playing time is my child going to get?" All we want is for our student athletes to get a fair amount of playing time. Tonya and I, like so many other parents, never questioned what would happen in the event of any type of emergency.

The day we got that fateful call, my first question upon arrival to the hospital was "What happened to Jordan?" My second question to the athletic trainers was "Has this ever happened to either of you before?"

There were too many things that Tonya and I had to learn in our accelerated crash course over those two weeks as Jordan was fighting for his life. We knew that this was an even larger scale problem, and that something had to be done.

The entire experience seemed surreal, almost like a dream. A new unknown met us at every turn. And every time Jordan's condition changed, we were met with a new, harsh reality. We were totally uneducated and clueless about what had just happened to Jordan. And the reality of our son's situation kept getting more significant as the days went by.

The entire time, I kept thinking to myself "If we don't know these things, how many other parents don't know these things?" I knew there had to be other parents who were as clueless as us. And I knew this wasn't the way any parent should find out about their son either.

When you aren't knowledgeable about something, it's no fault of your own. You just do not know what you don't know. It's that simple. However, when you're right in the thick of it and feel as though you *should have* known, it resonates differently. When this type of tragedy happens at home it's a totally different experience.

To do something about it, we decided to start a foundation. The idea for The Jordan McNair Foundation came rather easily.

I had already cofounded a non-profit organization with my business partner, Carlton Carrington and had a passion for outreach. Carlton was a coach and a mentor for Jordan as well. I've always had a spirit for advocacy and always want to make a difference in the lives of people who needed the most.

I guess you can say the idea grew from Jordan's massive, size 16 feet. Jordan always had bigger feet than the average teenager. We actually considered ourselves lucky when his feet stopped growing at a size 16. One would think that buying sneakers that size would be a problem. But, it wasn't. Someone was always sending him sneakers. It was like this unspoken code among big men.

One time, Tonya and Jordan were in Starbucks and, as usual, everyone was commenting on how tall my son was. When Tonya answered someone's question about his shoe size, a woman who approached her and said, "Excuse me, I overheard your comment about your son's shoe size. My son plays in the NBA and I've been looking for someone to give all of these sneakers he doesn't wear to." Like that, she would send boxes of barely worn shoes to us.

There were several stories like that. When Jordan started playing with an unlimited football program, I always encouraged him to give some of those shoes away to guys his size that had those big feet, too. Maybe that kid actually couldn't play without a new pair of sneakers. Sometimes, it is the littlest things that can make the biggest impact.

There wasn't a second thought about creating a legacy for Jordan that would make a difference in the world of youth and collegiate sports. We believe that Jordan had way too much living to do to leave here at such an early age.

The Jordan McNair Foundation was our way of keeping our son alive by promoting awareness, education, and prevention of heat-related injuries, and educating athletes and families on player safety. The pain I felt was so dark. I felt so unaware, I didn't want to waste any time. Jordan passed on June 13, 2018 The Jordan McNair Foundation was started on June 16, 2018.

Long before I knew if there were other families advocating for heat stroke injuries or fatalities, I knew we had to keep Jordan's legacy alive. I remember three days after Jordan passed my fiancé at the time and I were brainstorming on the name of The Jordan McNair Foundation. I remember saying, "Tonya and I have to educate other parents on what we had to learn the hard way."

I strongly believe that there is literally a lesson learned in every major life experience, good or bad. Even in times of tragedy like this, the takeaway for me as a loving father is that life is no way guaranteed and tomorrow is far from promised.

Jordan, whether we knew it or not at that time, was right where he was supposed to be in his life. We had accepted this, and we were grateful for the wonderful gift of a son who lived his best life in the 19 years that he was here. The foundation is how we keep his legacy alive. The heart of this foundation would be built on self-love, family, self-respect and self-discipline.

This foundation is how we would turn our pain into purpose. A non-profit organization's mission is to make a change, to cure an ill and to solve a problem in society. The Jordan McNair Foundation's mission is to promote awareness, educate, and advocate for parents and student athletes about heat-related injuries at the youth, high school and collegiate levels of sports.

We work to diminish the occurrence of heat-related injuries and improve player safety, and it's a goal with a real potential for a positive outcome. Heat-related injuries are 100% preventable—you just need to have the right tools to know how to stop them.

The Education Concept

As the story about what happened to Jordan began to unravel, we began to think about ways to develop awareness, education and prevention around heat-related injuries. Our mission came into focus; to educate everyone, parents, coaches, and mainly, student athletes on heat injury prevention. To give parents the knowledge we wish we would have had and that we wish we didn't have to learn.

As parents, we teach our children so many things from our experiences, the lessons from our playbook. As a father, I always wanted Jordan to be 100 times better than I was at his age. So, I, as a father always taught Jordan to stand up for what he believed in, to always be a leader, never a follower. I didn't want him to be impressionable like I was, or to make bad decisions like I did.

I always had a list of as much fatherly advice as I could muster up, things that would make life easier for him. However, I feel I neglected to teach him to speak up for himself, or his teammates, to his coaches. To *speak up* if he didn't feel comfortable doing something. I didn't teach him to listen to his body. These are such important things that didn't make my long list of fatherly advice and were things I didn't know could have saved my son's life.

We as parents don't tend to teach our children these things. We teach our student athletes be *coachable*. You hear about it all of the time, the great student athletes that are the "coachable" kids. We want our kids to listen to feedback, to be able to receive criticism constructively without taking it personally, to be willing to look at their own performance in order to improve it, and to generally be a super-bad-ass-go getter that works hard, but always responds to everything their adult coach tells them.

As hard as it is to agree with the definition "coachable" for a young student athlete, I do agree with some things. But I always thought "coaches coach and parents parent" paradigm was right. That is just the way it is, right?

"Coachable" for a student athlete to me, meant you listened to the coach all the time, even if coach is telling you to do something that makes you feel uncomfortable. Coaches like coachable kids, the ones that drink the Kool-Aid, don't speak up for themselves and who always pretend everything is OK.

They don't complain. They don't get tired. They don't get hurt. That's not a coachable kid, that's a robot without a voice. Just because an adult holds the title of "Coach" it doesn't mean that every word they say is gold. It also doesn't mean they know an athlete's body better than the athlete does.

We have to teach our children to speak up for themselves before we send them into these environments. If I'd taught Jordan to speak up for himself when he felt uncomfortable, I wouldn't be writing this book.

I am by no means placing blame on Jordan's teammates. But, if Jordan and his teammates had been educated about the signs, symptoms and prevention of all heat-related injuries, maybe they would have noticed there wasn't a cold-water tub on the practice field that day. Maybe they would have made a unified decision to not practice until one was brought out on the field.

If these athletes were empowered about exertional heat-related injuries, they could have noticed Jordan, or any other teammate, was having a heat stroke. But most kids aren't taught to be empowered—they are taught to be coachable.

What does this empowerment entail?

It means kids will know the number of student athletes who've passed away from a heat-related injury, so that they understand the severity of the condition and want to take action when they see the signs and symptoms in front of them.

It means all outdoor sports fields will have the proper safety equipment in place, including a cold-water tub, for all practices and games.

It means certified athletic trainers will be regarded as being as important as a referee at all youth sports events. It means all of these youth sports events will have a realistic emergency action plan in place and know how to use it.

All heat-related injuries can be 100% preventable, especially if this is what the world of youth sports looks like.

The more we are all educated about heat-related injuries, the safer our young people will be and there is nothing more important than that.

63 Days Later

For the 63 days following Jordan's death, we stayed completely silent. We didn't sit down for an interview, we never responded to the media and we never made an official statement. Jordan's story was one of the most talked about sports stories in 2018, and our initial silence spoke volumes. As hard as it was to stay silent, our legal team's strategy made an impact in this message that we were trying to get out to the world. I feel as though the national voice that we have now has been due to the tremendous amount of media attention surrounding our story.

Although we were silent, those 63 days were brutal. The media had been buzzing around since the night Jordan was injured, but we stayed silent. On June 13th, the day Jordan died, the media announced a full-scale investigation into his injury, but we stayed silent. The University of Maryland football staff made numerous reports to the media that only told a vastly different side of the story, and we stayed silent. But while we were silent, we were gathering information.

We were quickly finding out that Jordan was one of the *many* young student athletes who had died because of complications from a heat-related injury at the NCAA collegiate football level. All their stories were similar. They happened in the first few days of practice, with no cold-water tub on the field. The coaching staff didn't do their jobs, and as a result of that, the student athlete was injured or ultimately died from this error.

Jordan was a statistical fatality. He was one of the two to three collegiate football players that die during the first few days of conditioning drills. He was one of the more than 30 student athlete football players to die in the last 20 years. I spent my life trying to make sure my son didn't make the same mistakes I did. That he wouldn't become a statistic like I was. And yet he, did. He became a completely different type of statistic. He was a young man that was put in an environment where he died from preventable causes. It was a statistic I didn't even know existed, and one that most parents don't know about either.

Unfortunately, despite all of the attention surrounding Jordan, we lost another young man, Braeden Bradforth, that year. Braeden was a 19-year-old student athlete who died on August 18, 2018—the first day of practice. This was only a few months after Jordan. While Jordan's death garnered a great deal of interest it wasn't a new tale, it had happened over 30 times, yet we never heard of this type of injury. Jordan had been playing football on and off his entire life and we never knew about potentially fatal heat-related injuries. It was devastating to think that 30 other families went through the same pain we did. And I wanted to help.

Not speaking to the media and having to suppress our thoughts and feelings was extremely stressful. Watching our story in the news was like seeing a train wreck playing repeatedly, every single day. Every time a new article was written, and every time a new segment came on the news, it was another collision.

Many of Jordan's teammate's parents kept begging me to break my silence, to say something, but we didn't. It was challenging to not get caught up in everyone else's emotions, especially the other parents'. It could've been their son that went down that day with the same result. I understood *why* they wanted me to speak up, but I also understood why we were staying quiet.

I'm so grateful for our legal counsel and their support, strategy and constant reminder to only speak when it was advantageous to do so. I didn't really see at it the time, but we were building a national voice without saying anything. My only relief came from the comments section in articles from news outlets like *The Washington Post* and *Sports Illustrated*. I had become dependent on reading those comments for my own sanity. Even though I didn't agree with all of them, the majority of the readers said exactly what I was feeling every single day.

The court of public opinion has a certain weight to it at times like these. People were angry, people were shocked, and we could all agree that when young person loses their life to a preventable tragedy in any arena, that something must be done.

My goal was to start speaking, around the country, and to start bringing my message to people, like me, who didn't know about the risks of heat-related injuries. As I was trying to get on the public speaking circuit to share our story, an agent from a prominent speaker's bureau told me:

"Mr. McNair, Americans don't want to hear about the negative side of sports."

While this door closed in front of me, Heather Dinich's article opened a different door. When Heather's article dropped, I instantly saw how college football would be changed. And the heads started to roll. The very next day, the University of Maryland started suspending members of the coaching staff. I knew this was going to be bigger than I imagined, and Jordan's death was going to be the catalyst to set it all off.

During those 63 days, so many reporters were calling and knocking on my and Tonya's doors. Our only initial comment was always that there was "no comment at this time."

The press was aggressive. We stayed silent, and we asked all of our family members to not give comments either.

The media can do so many things in your favor, or they can do so many things to your detriment. A lot of times, we as people who have experienced a tragedy speak emotionally to the media too soon. Journalist are extremely creative in using your words of vulnerability against you. This is why our initial armor of protection was to simply stick with the "no comment" phrase, over and over again.

Most families start talking to the media about the death of their loved one right away. It all goes well until someone ask the question, "What happened?" Many times, at that point, the family doesn't know. They don't have all of the facts about what really occurred. I didn't want that to be the case with us. If I was going to make a public statement about the death of my son, I wanted to have a statement that was going to make an impact and I wanted to have all of my facts straight.

Jordan passed away on June 13, 2018, our first interview was on August 16, 2018, the week after Heather Dinich's ESPN article debuted.

Tonya and I rode the train from Baltimore to New York the evening before we were to appear publicly on "Good Morning America." It had been 63 days and I was nearly overjoyed at the idea of finally being able to say something in Jordan's honor. Our words had to be thorough and precise from this point on.

I was surprised to find that the major programs like "Good Morning America" and "The Today Show" all compete with headline breaking news. If one affiliate airs a story, the others don't want it. We had "Good Morning America." This was our platform and we had 6 minutes to make an impact.

The day started extremely early I remember we met our legal team in the hotel lobby at 6 AM and walked across the street into GMA's studio by 6:30. Tonya, myself and our attorney, Hassan Murphy, sat down for an interview with Michael Strahan. Michael is a former NFL player and someone who could understand the type of impact this could have on the world of college football. Our story didn't have any racial, cultural or financial barriers. We all have student athletes as sons, daughters, nieces and nephews, this affected us all.

After we finished the interview with "Good Morning America" we traveled through Manhattan to do and interview with Heather Dinich from ESPN. We arrived at the Algonquin Hotel, one of the oldest hotels and historic landmarks in Manhattan, ready to sit down with the woman who helped blow the lid off this whole thing.

Heather's 45-minute interview was extremely emotional. The questions she asked regarding our feelings every juncture of the way and reliving the entire experience, was challenging. It had only been 63 days; the wounds were still fresh.

It was hard not to break down in tears, Tonya is an emotional person, once her tears start flowing, I'd be giving everything to hold my own back and stay focused on getting our message out.

Every time I speak publicly about Jordan's story, I'm drained emotionally. It is as if I'm running off of pure adrenalin when telling it, even as I write this. Going through the events that first day in New York took us to some dark places. We had been in the media daily since Jordan was injured, but we had never spoken. We never had an opportunity to grieve and it didn't look like an opportunity to do so was anywhere in sight.

I kept thinking we are in a place that the parents of those 30 kids have never been in. We were given an opportunity to bring awareness to this in ways they were not. We were given a national platform to give a voice to those that didn't have one. We didn't ask to be here, and most certainly did not want to be here.

If this was our platform, we had to use it to make a difference in the world. We knew we had to prevent another family from experiencing the feeling of losing a child this way. If this is what we were being called to do, we were up for the task.

Tonya and I needed a mental break after that interview. Our next meeting later that evening was with the producers of HBO's *Real Sports*. The plan was to meet our legal team back at the hotel that evening in route to our dinner meeting.

We walked through Manhattan attempting to get some fresh air, both caught up in our own thoughts as we strolled along looking at the sights of the city.

I had been to New York thousands of times, however that day, it looked different. Everyone in Manhattan always seems to move so quickly—heads down, laser-focused on getting to their next destination. I felt as if I were floating through this sea of busy people, completely disconnected from the chaos around me—and I got the break I so desperately needed.

Later that evening we were in another black SUV in route to our dinner with the producers from HBO's *Real Sports*. I don't remember what I ate. In fact, nothing about the food stuck out at all. But I do remember the Midtown location, right across from Bryant Park. There were hundreds of people doing yoga there that evening. I was thinking this is where I should be taking classes with hundreds of people.

I was confident at least one other person would be as bad as me attempting a Reverse Warrior pose. I let my mind wander to those hundreds of people relaxing with their yoga poses. It was as though for the first time, after getting through those interviews in the morning, that I didn't feel so overwhelmed. I knew we could get through this.

We were informed that this story would be "College Football Workout Deaths." I'm sure it was already in production, however, Jordan's story likely placed a sense of urgency on it. The thought that there was an entire segment on college football players dying snapped me back into attention.

It was ridiculous that there is enough content to air an entire episode on players dying during their college football workouts. But this is the reality we are living in. Death was being normalized in the world of collegiate football.

We had another interview lined up for the next day—a segment with CNN and Erica Hill. I was still learning to be precise and impactful in the few minutes we had to tell our story. I was still working on mastering my interview skills, and learning how to tell our story tactfully, and without losing composure.

On the train ride home, I was finally able to take a breath. The experience was physically and emotionally draining. The world had now heard our story. We had broken our silence and finally gotten the chance to tell our truth. We brought attention to heat-related injuries and told millions of Americans what we intended to do about them through our mission of awareness, education and prevention.

I wanted nothing more than to get home and go get some sleep, because the real work was about to start.

Empowerment Through Education

When Jordan passed away, Tonya and I were totally unaware of the statistics of exertional heat injuries. In fact, we had never even heard of this condition. As our continued education into the world of heat-related injuries began, we realized that Jordan's tragedy wasn't the first of its kind. Yet we had never heard of the many athletes who succumbed to similar complications. It is as though their stories were only relevant to their families and the schools they attended. Their message wasn't reaching beyond their own communities, even to us as parents of fellow student athletes.

I did not know many of these players, not even Korey Stringer. And I had never heard of The Korey Stringer Institute. Before Jordan, Korey Stringer was the most recognized athlete who died from complications related to heat stroke. Korey had been in the NFL for six seasons. He was a father, a former Ohio State player and a first-round draft pick.

In 2001, Korey was at his first day of the Minnesota Vikings training camp and couldn't finish the first day of drills. He sat out from exhaustion during the afternoon session. Determined to complete practice the next day, Korey showed up to camp, practiced in full pads, and vomited three times on the field. Later that afternoon, when Korey was admitted to the St. Joseph's Mayo Health System Hospital, his body temperate was 108° F.

He passed away that night. Beyond tragic, his death was senseless. Despite Korey being in the NFL, and despite his tragedy happening 17 years before Jordan's—not much in the world of player safety had changed since his untimely passing.

There were other players, too. Names I had never heard of until I began my harrowing dive into the world of heat-related injuries. Names like Marquese Meadow, the 19-year-old freshman at Morgan State University who died from complications of a heat stroke while his team was running punishment drills. He was running, as a punishment, for over an hour in the heat.

By the time he collapsed and was rushed to a nearby hospital, his body temperature was 106.6° F. Marquese died just four years before Jordan, at a school not far from where we live, yet I didn't even know his name until my own son passed.

But soon enough, all of these names became relevant to me. They were also athletes, sons and people who had succumbed to the same type of preventable injury as Jordan did. And their deaths never needed to happen. The more I researched, the farther down the rabbit hole I went.

I learned about player after player who fell victim to heat stroke, while under the supervision of a coach or trainer. I wanted to learn as much information as I could. While I couldn't save my son, I knew that I could help future athletes by finally placing the necessary attention on these injuries, and how they can be avoided.

The first person I ever spoke to that really understood the weight of our tragedy was Marquese Meadow's mom, Benita. I remember the first thing she told me was that she felt as though she didn't have a voice. She didn't know who to blame beyond the coach who had them running the punishment drill. Tonya and I would refuse to feel the same level of impotence. I didn't want us to feel as though we didn't have a voice. I wanted us to actually make a difference, and we were determined to do so in this fight to keep student athletes safe.

The list of athletes who have succumbed to this condition doesn't stop with Korey and Marquese. It is a long list and one that is painful to look at. On this list you will see a young high school football athlete, a cheerleader and a female basketball player who lost their lives due to complications from heat-related injuries, and all since Jordan passed. Tonya and I relive the pain every time we see a name added to the list and every time we send flowers to the funerals of these young people.

Since the year 2000, 30 student athletes have died from over strenuous collegiate conditioning drills or workouts. Thirty dead players in 18 years, all in college. It's beyond comprehension, yet the statistics only get worse. On top of these senseless deaths, it is predicted that we will lose an additional two to three student athletes every year at the NCAA collegiate level because of heat stroke or a heat-related injury.

As many as three young, promising college students lost every year to something that is entirely preventable. This doesn't even include the number of student athletes that have died at the AAU and high school levels, who didn't even get an opportunity to live out their college dreams.

You would think that the first death of one of these student athletes would have sprung the NCAA into action. That this association, who is dedicated to the development of collegiate athletes would mandate that all college programs have the proper preventative equipment in place. But they didn't. After the loss of Korey Stringer in 2001, the NFL took notice and began implementing proper prevention systems throughout the league. Yet despite all the deaths at lower levels of play, these preventative measures have yet to trickle down to help our young people.

Each of these tragedies is as heartbreaking as the next. Each story is unique, just as each young athlete is unique. But each story has one common denominator; *there was not a cold-water tub present on the field when the injury happened.*

Imagine the sinking feeling I felt, the first time I went into a Tractor Supply Store and saw a Rubber Maid stock tub sitting on display. Also known as a cold-water tub, this 150-gallon bin was on sale for just $129.00. That's it, $129.00, and you can get it at nearly any home improvement store. This same 150-gallon tub can easily fit a 6'5, 300-pound lineman in it, with more than enough room for ice to cool him down. And here it was, staring me down with a sale sticker on the front.

My thoughts immediately switched from disbelief to frustration. If a cold-water tub had been on the field or nearby at practice, we wouldn't have over 30 dead student athletes in the past 18 years. How could something so simple be overlooked over *30 times* at the college level?

I felt angry. But I also felt empowered and determined to put an end to this nonsense. I knew that real change not only rested on my own empowerment, but on the empowerment of others. And the only way to empower others to take action was to educate them in the same way I was educated.

I felt a need to enlighten every single parent, student athlete and coach so that they may identify the signs and symptoms of heat-related injuries and step up to stop them from happening, so they can understand the facts that we didn't and ask the questions we didn't know we needed to ask.

When parents are educated on the potential risks associated with youth sports, *they* are empowered. When coaches and trainers know the necessary safety equipment that should always be on the field, *they* are empowered. When our student athletes know the signs and symptoms of heat-related injuries, *they* are empowered. And as you read this, I hope you will be empowered too.

With this information, student athletes, parents and coaches can all work together to make sure that everyone playing sports is doing so safely. No parent can be at every practice. No athlete can watch his teammate during every drill. No coach can keep his eye on every player during conditioning. But the more we all know about these heat-related injuries, the better prepared we will all be to look out for each other, to notice the signs in one another, and to help finally put an end to these senseless and preventable deaths.

Just like every other part of sports, it requires teamwork. It is not a burden that just one player, coach or parent can bear—it is a change that needs to infiltrate through the entire culture of youth sports. Every time one person is able to stand up and say something and bring attention to the potential symptoms of heat-related injury, it can make a difference. It can save a life. When Tonya and I started The Jordan McNair Foundation, our goal was to do just this. And it all starts with basic player safety.

One of the immediate takeaways when Jordan passed was the feeling that I taught him so many things to help him be successful in life, but the one thing I didn't teach him was to speak up for himself if he didn't feel comfortable. I take responsibility for that. Even among all the fatherly advice that I gave him over the years, I didn't tell him "always listen to your body son." I didn't tell him "If your body tells you to stop, then stop."

I wish I would have told him that listening to his own body was more important than listening to a coach. In fact, I always, like so many other fathers, taught him the opposite. I taught him to be coachable, to be tough and to suck it up. How did I forget to tell him to listen to his body in the midst of all that fatherly advice?

I missed that. I didn't tell him "Jordan you don't have to put 1000 percent effort out at every practice or workout." I wasn't worried about the potential safety issues with giving maximum effort. I, like many parents, thought giving this type of effort was only going to make him better. I take blame for not empowering Jordan as well as I should have about something he loved as much as football.

The more educated we all are, the safer everyone will be. I often think about what it would've looked like if all of Jordan's teammates were educated about the awareness and prevention of heat-related injuries the day Jordan was injured. Would there have been a different outcome? Maybe in a perfect world, but now I can only speculate.

If they did know, what would they have said? What questions would they have asked? Would they have stood up to their coaches?

"Coach, we don't see a cold-water tub on the field."

"Coach, we're not practicing until we get a cold-water tub."

"Coach, my teammate doesn't look well, he may be having a heat stroke."

Would they have told their coaches that on humid days, the likelihood of heat injury is higher? Would they have looked up the Wet Bulb Globe Thermometer Reading? Would they have known that the proper acclimation period for athletes returning to practice is 10-14 days? Would they have known to look at their urine to determine if they were properly hydrated?

We will never know.

I'm not saying someone, particularly Jordan's teammates, could have saved my son. None of them, like so many student athletes, were probably educated on this type of common injury. However, it looks completely different when they are.

Kids are kids, no matter how tall, how much they weigh or how big their feet are. And at the D1 college level, they are literally just that, giant kids. However, we have to educate them on the things that Tonya and I didn't teach Jordan. What we as parents didn't know at that time. The lesson that may have saved my son's life when he needed it the most. That simple lesson was to always listen to your body, before you listen to anyone else—and when your body tells you to stop, you stop.

PART V

June 13, 2019
One Year Later

Jordan passed June 13, 2018. June 13 was quickly creeping up in 2019 and we had just celebrated the inaugural Jordan McNair Annual Golf Classic. It was a huge success. Due to the potential direction of litigation at that time, we were somewhat dormant in our advocacy efforts. I'd been speaking to a few local high school football programs that I had relationships with, however, we were still figuring out what the best way to honor Jordan would be.

I also felt that if we didn't do something meaningful that day, it would be unbearable. I had to come up with something to fill the void to protect everyone in the family's emotional well-being or else it I didn't know how we would all make it through. I wanted to honor him in a way so big, and so impactful, that there was no way any of us could be sad that day.

We were already preparing for our first annual Jordan McNair Golf Tournament when I had the idea for a health and wellness sports clinic. My head at that time was filled with so many Jordan McNair ideas, sports camps, golf tournaments, speaking engagements, more fundraising events and whatever else I could think of to continue to build the brand around his name and story.

A lot of this was new to me but I've always been the guy who thinks that no project is too big. If I'm not nervous enough about a project, it's not big enough. I do know that the key to success when chartering into the unknown with certain things is to surround yourself with intelligent, experienced people who are subject matter experts in their own niche.

Our golf committee was comprised of a few good friends and family members who were more experienced golfers than I was and had put together golf tournaments for other fundraisers in the past. I was the total novice, however, those experienced intelligent folks I surrounded myself with put together a majorly successful inaugural event.

The weather was great that day, after a few days of rain prior. The sun was shining bright, the course was dry, and we felt as though every golfer left feeling they had a memorable experience—and would want to return and support the next tournament we held. This was one of those Jordan-smiling-down moments I like to talk about. It just felt like his spirit was all over the place during the tournament, big and bright and full of life.

I knew that I had to think fast on the health and wellness clinic, because this time the previous year, Jordan was in the hospital fighting for his life. The golf tournament was May 31, 2019 the day before the anniversary of his liver transplant on June 1, 2018. These dates and time frames were so significant and they were what motivated me to stay on task.

The year before at this time, we were praying for Jordan's recovery and less than 365 days later, we were planning charitable events in his honor. I knew a lot of the people I needed to speak to would be attending the golf tournament that day, so while Tonya and I were riding around shaking hands and taking pictures with all of the golfers I was pitching the idea of the sports clinic. They say a lot of deals are made on the golf course, I made some of my most important ones to date that day.

I knew that I needed a big enough location to do the clinic and chose Jordan's high school alma mater, the McDonogh School. We had support from the headmaster and athletic staff. The new head football coach, and one of Jordan's mentors, Hakeem Sule stepped in to help me out tremendously with the logistics. I had also enlisted UMD's new head coach Mike Locksley to join the project.

The goal was to send some players to an elementary school in DC that day. The other group of the guys, mostly ones who played with Jordan went to McDonogh. My idea to make our camp unique from a regular sports clinic was to invite parents and coaches as well. I'd taken Jordan to so many sports clinics and football combines over the years. I've only sat in the stands with the rest of the other parents who chose to hang around watching our kids participate. There was no education or information regarding player safety or anything. I didn't want that for us. The Jordan McNair Health and Wellness Sports Clinic would be an experience for everyone who attended.

I had only 12 days after the golf tournament to put something monumental together and was ready to make it work. We had a location, we had the UMD Terrapins support, I had someone do a flyer for the event that we started circulating, I started working on a training curriculum with the help of our Harvard graduate cousin, who's a stickler for these sorts of things.

She has been our consigliere in the non-profit arena and spiritual advisor throughout this entire experience. She is also quick to point to her Harvard degree on the wall to put me back in place when I get locked in on an idea. It's funny how it works every time.

I knew that we had to educate parents and coaches beyond those questions of "Can my child play?" and "Why isn't my child playing?" The age group for the camp was 8-14 years of age and parents were still at a point where they could be educated out of the "coaches coach and parents parent," mindset.

All we needed at this point was a certified athletic trainer to do the training and some cold-water tubs to donate.

Finding a trainer was more time consuming than I anticipated. My information on athletic trainers was limited at that time. One call led to a guy who was strength and conditioning trainer and he turned me on to a company that made an inflatable tub, which we ordered to donate to the each of the sports programs who attended. Coach Sule stepped in and enlisted McDonogh's athletic trainer, Ashley, to work with us that day and things really began shaping up. We had a backup plan in place, our strategic advisory team sent out press releases to the media, and we were ready to go.

We started the morning of June 13, 2019 at the University of Maryland, in front of the Gossett Football building. That rainy afternoon when we pulled up for Jordan's visit seemed like a lifetime ago. The day started with a tree planting ceremony in honor of Jordan. There was still a lot of pain being back in the football building, but the support from University of Maryland's athletic department and football program was a step in the right direction. I was happy they were honoring a teammate and friend.

The tree planting ceremony was a positive start to the day as we received warm hugs from the entire football team, new coaching staff, members of the athletic department and the school's president. It felt oddly reassuring to see new men in charge of this program we once had so much hope for.

I was feeling nervous about that day's events. By then I noticed, whenever I'm feeling nervous, it means I'm pushing myself in the right direction, and it's a great sign that my project will have an impact. By that time, we had realized the sun wouldn't come out and we would be indoors that day. The weather forecast called for rain and thunderstorms but it slowed down just at the right time so we could get started.

As the media and hundreds of student athletes, coaches and parents all came together in McDonogh's gymnasium, I could feel the positivity in the air. Seeing everyone in Jordan's number 79 t-shirts made me truly see and feel the magnitude of what we were doing and what these camps could potentially evolve into. I had 10 microphones hooked up to my t-shirt that day as I gave interviews to the media about our mission and what we were looking to accomplish. By this time, I was much more experienced with using the short amount of time I had to make a clear and impactful statement.

While the kids were downstairs in one gym with the Maryland football players, parents and coaches stayed in the other gym with us. We had officially started our very first training session on the signs, symptoms and prevention of heat-related injuries. Ashley, our athletic trainer that day, talked everyone through heat-related injuries, while I chimed in as a parent, asking questions and encouraging others to do so as well.

The team moms, parents and coaches were all interactive during the session. As Ashley engaged the crowd and showcased how to use a cold-water tub in the event of a heat-related injury, I could see the light bulbs go off in people's minds. To see these basic fundamentals click so clearly and to see our audience truly understand what prevention entailed and how to step into action when a heat-related injury occurs, was priceless. I'd rather a parent be just as educated about heat-related injuries and a team's emergency action plan, as the coaching staff their child plays for. I'd rather a parent runs on the field 100 times to save any child playing, than to have a preventable injury happen because there was no preparation, and I could see all of the parents around us getting it.

After our session, we all went down to the gym with the kids and players watching everyone having the time of their lives running, doing drills, and enjoying sports the way they're meant to be enjoyed. How could Tonya or I be somber this day? As everyone gathered together in that gym, I spoke about the significance of speaking up for yourself. I made sure every student athlete in that gym knew to speak up if they ever felt uncomfortable and most importantly start listening to their bodies when they tell them to stop.

Our first Jordan McNair Health and Wellness Sports Clinic was a success. I know our son was with us that entire day saying, "Good job, Mom and Dad." I couldn't have imagined a better day honoring my son than with a day of sports that were fun and safe for everyone.

I was overcome with excitement. I felt triumph and joy and as though we had just celebrated a major victory with our inaugural sports clinic. I beelined to the cemetery to share the news of our day with Jordan. I couldn't have been more thrilled to tell him every detail of the day. Then suddenly, the rain stopped and a faint rainbow appeared right as the sun started to set. No, there was no way we could be sad that day. No way to be sad at all.

Making a Difference

With all the media coverage surrounding the health and wellness clinic, the foundation's phone started to ring off the hook. A few organizations asked me to do trainings locally, and thanks to the power of social media, I had people from across the nation calling to ask about speaking engagements.

I was slowly starting to see that we had a national voice in the advocacy of heat-related awareness, education and prevention. However, we weren't the only ones who were making a difference. There is the Zach Martin Foundation and the Polsenberg Charity in Florida, run by the parents of Zach Martin Polsenberg who passed in 2017.

Zach was also running sprints with his high school football team when he collapsed and suffered an exertional heat stroke. This organization is making a big difference in promoting awareness in Florida and helping to bring new safety procedures to students at the high school level.

When I received a call from Dr. Steven Horowitz at Team Safe Sport, I realized this wasn't just a problem in the sport of football, but in all outside sports that student athletes play in during spring and summer. Baseball, softball, soccer, rugby, lacrosse, field hockey and basketball; these injuries happen in sports of all types and to athletes of all ages.

Then, on Friday of that week, divine order took over. I was lacing my sneakers up for a morning run at about 6:30 AM, watching the news for the weather forecast. I heard the weatherman say that it would be a Code Orange that day— temperatures were unhealthy for sensitive groups. During these alerts, children, inactive adults and people with respiratory disease such as asthma should limit their outdoor activity.

I instinctively made a post to our Facebook page with a simple plea.

"Parents and coaches, it's a Code Orange today. Please be smart if your student athletes are practicing outside. Keep them hydrated. And moms, please commit to taking a bag of ice to every practice. If the sports program your child plays is an outside sport and you don't have a cold-water tub, reach out to The Jordan McNair Foundation, we'll donate one ASAP #100percentpreventable."

My idea got brighter, I went back and put the foundation number in the post. But I didn't think to add in the state of Maryland only or in the DMV only. I just wanted to get

216

the message out. I was completely unaware that Tonya made a profound post on Twitter too. That evening, the foundation phone number started to ring with callers from California, Nebraska, Florida, Indiana and all over the country. People saw our post and they wanted to help keep their kids safe.

The response was overwhelming, and we literally had just one cold-water tub left after our first sports clinic. After that post, we donated over 200 cold-water tubs across the nation from Alaska to Florida. We donated to rugby teams, baseball teams, soccer teams, football teams and track and field teams. We got cold-water tubs to the youth, AAU, high school and collegiate levels of sports programs. Who knew that this offhanded post, where I almost forgot to post the number of our foundation, would help so many people?

If you're reading this, no matter where you are, The Jordan McNair Foundation will donate a cold-water tub to your team right away. It doesn't matter where you are located or what outdoor sport you play—one more cold-water tub could save one more life.

Not only did we donate cold-water tubs to all of these programs, we spoke to parents, coaches and mainly athletic trainers who consistently complained there wasn't enough money in their budget for this piece of safety equipment. Money for an inexpensive lifesaving piece of equipment like this should *always* be available.

We asked everyone who received a cold-water tub to visit our website and view an instructional video from one of our partners at the Zach Martin Foundation, post a pic on Twitter with the tub and send us a team jersey for our office walls. Nothing makes me happier than seeing those team jerseys lining our walls—a constant reminder of all of the kids who will be able to play the sports they love *safely*.

Advocating for Change

I'll be the first to admit that I never thought I would be a guy holding up signs, or advocating for a cause I wholeheartedly believed in. But this is what my purpose is now, to advocate for change and to help make sure our kids can stay safe while playing youth sports.

I remember when the coaches from Maryland sat at our kitchen table a few days before National Signing Day. We asked questions about Jordan's well-being and playing time. They told us if Jordan came to spring practice well-conditioned, he'd get an opportunity. We were assured, "Your child will be safe here, we'll take care of him as if he was our own."

Of course, we trusted and believed these men. Unfortunately, that wasn't the case, and when Jordan complained and was in visible distress during conditioning workouts, the coaches didn't take care of him. We didn't think to ask about an emergency action plan if Jordan or any of his teammates got hurt on the field. Like so many parents, we didn't think to ask what policies were in place, or what guarantees were in place if he couldn't play football again.

Most importantly, we didn't think to research beyond our information source—the two men sitting before us. While Jordan was in a hospital bed for two weeks fighting for his life from a preventable injury, we continuously asked ourselves "What questions didn't we ask?"

I remember thinking early on in our journey that getting a law passed in Jordan's name would be a great way to honor my son's legacy. I felt strongly that Jordan was a martyr in this whole situation. He died by doing something he truly loved and believed in. He would eat, sleep and breathe football, and ultimately, football was how he died.

The Jordan McNair Safe and Fair Play Act will educate and advocate for the safety of all student athletes while attending higher level educational institutions. We, as parents, should feel confident that our children will always be safe when we send them away to college. We should feel assured that college will develop them into better young adults, preparing them for life, and a chance to play at a professional level of sports.

The NCAA has a mere $10,000.00 life insurance policy on all student athletes in the event of a tragedy. A student athlete's life is worth very little in the world of profitable collegiate sports and this must change. College football is a big machine, one that makes a lot of money and has a lot of influence, and we must make sure that our young men don't get crushed in this machine as the wheels keep on spinning.

The more empowered student athletes are in their true value and self-worth, the stronger their voice becomes in the decisions that are made regarding their safety, education and overall well-being. This Act will aim to bring that protection to student athletes like Jordan.

As I continued to educate myself on heat-related injuries, I didn't really see what safety laws were in place regarding these injuries and player safety. I was confident that locally and in the world of college sports, people would have some name recognition when Jordan's name was mentioned. I did know that in the bigger picture, I wanted to set up Jordan McNair Foundation offices in various states, as advocates for heat-related injuries and other player safety issues. I also knew that the city of Baltimore and the state of Maryland would be our best launching pads to establish this type of impact.

For me, the daily news is the best way to keep up with everything that's going on in the world. I still get Google alerts every time Jordan's name is mentioned in any news article. One evening while watching the news, I watched a story again mentioning the safety of student athletes in Baltimore City. Jordan was becoming the unofficial poster boy for student athlete safety across the nation.

The recognition between Jordan and player safety had become one in the same.

This is when I learned that Brandon Scott, the President of the Baltimore City Council was leading a sports safety bill to help protect young people in the city from heat-related injuries. I immediately got on the phone and called Zach McDaniels, our strategic advisor on our legal team and asked him to get us a meeting with Brandon. Zach has been instrumental in scheduling all of our local and national media interviews. Within days, Tonya and I were walking into city hall to meet with Brandon Scott in person.

Throughout this process, I've continued to learn how to choose my words carefully and to make sure I can get my point across within minutes. While meeting with Brandon, I told him, point blank, that I thought the safety bill would be more impactful if Jordan's name was added to it. I had gotten my point across in that 5-7-minute window before Brandon was whisked away to another meeting. I was given a copy of the draft of the bill and our input was welcomed if we wanted to make any additions.

My input was to have every coach that the bill applied to be trained on the signs, symptoms and prevention of all heat-related injuries. They should also watch the two instructional videos on how to use a cold-water tub we have on The Jordan McNair Foundation website. One of the videos is from one of our partners in player safety advocacy, Team Safe Sports.

This video educates viewers about heat-related injuries, acclimation periods of student athletes while practicing in warm and humid conditions, proper hydration and other sports injury preventive measures. The other video is from our advocacy partners at The Zach Martin Foundation. It educates viewers how to use a cold-water tub and other cooling techniques in the event of a heat-related injury.

Finally, I added that there should be mandatory for all schools and recreation centers in Baltimore City to have stationary cold-water tub where outside sports are played. This would cover more than 500 locations.

That evening of October 7, 2019 the bill went before the Baltimore City Council to add Jordan's name to this Safety Act. The vote was unanimous. Once it's signed by the mayor, it will take effect in the year 2020.

The Jordan McNair Youth Athletic Protection Act

For the purpose of establishing certain protections for youth athletes using Baltimore City Department of Recreations and Parks Facilities: requiring that youth athletic coaches complete certain training; requiring that youth athletes be removed from athletic play if they are suspected to have sustained medical conditions; requiring that the Department of Recreation and Parks make an automated external defibrillator available to certain youth sports programs defining certain terms; establishing certain penalties; providing for a special effective date; and generally relating to youth protection.

Our partnership with Baltimore City Department of Recreation and Parks will ensure that all coaches are trained , those cold-water tubs get to those recreation centers and fields, as well as implement the laws that will make all parents feel comfortable with the safety of their child playing youth sports in Baltimore City.

We made a difference in Baltimore, and I continue to urge people from all over the country to make a difference in their hometowns as well. making a difference in Baltimore was only the first step. Next, we had to take things to the state level.

One May morning, I was reading an article about House Bill 876 regarding the safety of student athletes at the University of Maryland and other state colleges in the area. Then, I had an idea. I immediately sent the delegate at the helm of this an email requesting we attach Jordan's name to the bill.

Good Morning, Delegate Hettleman,

A note of thanks for introducing House Bill 876 after the unfortunate loss of my son Jordan McNair. His passing was not in vain when we as parents and family see the impact that he's having on college athletics.

Interesting thing, Delegate Hettleman is that this had happen 30 plus times in the NCAA before Jordan and never made it to national headlines. I believe that Jordan's mission in life was to make change in the world of college athletics. Empowering athletes with the power and freedom to speak out when their bodies tell them to stop or when they feel uncomfortable in any environment as well the playing field.

We always knew Jordan was special and would change the world we just didn't know how'd he do it.

As parents we prepare, motivate, and support our children to be whatever they want to be with a touch of our influence somewhere in the recipe for a successful life. My goal was always to be a good example for my son. I never realized while I was teaching him, he was preparing me for this mission to save lives in his honor.

Delegate how do we go about attaching Jordan's name to House Bill 876?

Thank you again, warmest regards
Martin McNair

Delegate Hettleman responded immediately with words of moral support and encouragement as a mother of two. It put me at ease. She had also thought about adding Jordan's name to this bill, but out of respect of our privacy, had held back. She didn't know our grief had transformed into energy and we were charging forward full steam ahead to make a difference of bringing awareness to this cause.

One month later, Tonya and I were walking into a meeting, feeling Jordan's love smiling down on us, supporting what we were doing in his honor to save others. I still get those moments when he does that. So many of our life experiences since his passing have been spiritually intervening. It's like he right there with us in so many different scenarios, it's hard *not* to feel his presence some days.

Our initial meeting with Delegate Hettleman started the legislation discussions of attaching Jordan's name to House Bill 876. The Jordan McNair Act sounds much more impactful than a house bill or a senate bill with a number attached. Let this law have a thought provoking and meaningful name of a young man who meant something significant to the world attached to it.

Hopefully, this law will be acknowledged by Jordan's peers and save the lives of many other student athletes in the years to come. That House Bill 876 was passed in 2019. We would go on to testify in January of 2020 before the members of the Education, Health and Environmental Affairs Committee at the State House in Annapolis, Maryland to request that

Jordan's name be added to the now Senate Bill 27. Tonya and I sat before that committee as I read our statement.

As parents who lost a child to a preventable injury, we couldn't ask ourselves enough times "what didn't we prepare Jordan for or protect him from?" No parent willingly or knowingly sends their child off to any higher-educational institution for them to be bullied, threatened, or to become a target of any discriminatory behavior.

We think as parents to prepare them to speak up for themselves in any uncomfortable situation on the field, classroom, and socially without the fear of retribution or worse. Jordan's death has highlighted examples of where his fellow student athletes didn't feel safe speaking up in defense of a teammate in fear of retribution, loss of scholarship, or worse.

No parent or student athlete should feel that their personal safety is at risk or the safety of their child could possibly be taken for granted. Especially when we trust a higher-level educational institution to develop them into future thought leaders and prepare them for life.

Senate Bill 27, named after Jordan McNair, will not only keep our young student athletes safe and empowered at these higher-level educational institutions but will also keep his legacy alive forever.

Martin McNair and Tonya Wilson
Founders of The Jordan McNair Foundation

Again, the vote was unanimous. I was still a novice to the legislation process. However, I was quickly seeing that state laws are respected and give credibility to the name and the cause that you're advocating for.

The goal with getting this law passed at the state level was to create a line of communication that empowers student athletes to bravely discuss their concerns and have a voice to do so.

If young people feel uncomfortable for whatever reason, there should be a system in place to express that, without fear of any negative consequences. We look at the media daily and at so many scandals that happened within college sports programs. These are scandals that may have been prevented if there was an option to anonymously voice fear or concern.

Unfortunately, we live in a reactionary society where it takes a tragedy to happen before we react with systems of prevention. However, it's never too late to try to do *something* to prevent it from happening again. This senate committee meeting was our something.

As Tonya and I sat at the table in front of this senate committee, comprised of senators and other political representatives, I realized that we were making progress in our mission to be heard. As I testified in front of this committee, my every word was filled with passion and purpose for honoring Jordan. Tonya had to tap me on my leg to let me know to wrap it up. I felt confident I made an impression that day as she whispered, "you killed it, good job."

I've visited the State House in Annapolis on several occasions during 2020. I have been speaking about the importance of Jordan's name being attached to one more popular sport related house and senate bill. The goal of getting Jordan's name attached wasn't the main objective, it was to not let his death be in vain. I want his name to have the power, credibility and persuasion to influence change to make a difference not only in the state of Maryland, but across all states in our country.

I'm often glad that it was Jordan's mission to become a catalyst for change, because this has become a full-time job for me. I am fortunate that as a business owner, I already had the flexibility and time to advocate for this mission on a full-time basis. My first few experiences in the legislation and policy process have been a learning experience to say the least.

Each time I get a little better and learn a little more. But every time I'm in the State House in Annapolis, my experiences are filled with firm handshakes and words of encouragement to keep fighting for change. And so, I do.

PART VI

Mastering the Mundane

When I was in prison, I learned about the importance of mastering the most mundane acts as I prepared myself to return to society. They were simple, yet essential to my development as a human being, particularly as I began to focus on finding success on the other side. Mastering the mundane changed my life, and it can change others' lives too.

Since I have been working with The Jordan McNair Foundation, I have had the opportunity to speak to so many athletes from around the country and I always ask them the most basic questions.

Do they wash their hands every time they use the restroom? Do they put a seatbelt on every time they get in the car? Do they say please and thank you often? Do they make their beds every morning? That last one always gets a bit of a laugh.

This series of questions gets them thinking. Then I ask a simple "why?" And their answers vary from what it's what their parents taught them to do to it's the "right" thing to do. These behaviors unknowingly are preventive to keep them safe and to develop them into adults with good habits.

All of their answers are correct, because there is no right or wrong answer on *why* you do it. These behaviors that so many people take for granted can quickly become a habit with enough repetition. They're just things *you do.*

As any elite athlete will tell you, real success often comes down to the boring fundamentals—the mundane skills that produce better results in the long run. The best of the best do more than show up to a game with a good mental attitude, and they do more than work out long and hard in the gym.

Successful athletes educate themselves on injury, they hydrate properly with water, they stretch, watch film, they prepare and study. They become a student of the sport that they're playing. They do all of these boring fundamentals over and over again until they become second nature, then they practice them and practice them some more. These habits become so ingrained in their DNA—they just start doing them without thinking.

A successful athlete always makes good decisions on and off the field. The consistency of the two always shows in your performance. The inconsistency sticks out even more.

But what if personal safety habits became one of these fundamentals? What if they became one of those mundane habits that students engage in without thinking? How successful, and safe, could athletes be then?

I like to teach student athletes how to use the W.A.I.T. method when making good decisions, especially off the field. W.A.I.T. stands for "What Am I Thinking?" I encourage students to W.A.I.T before the act emotionally or erratically. When you ask yourself, "What am I thinking?" it gives you an opportunity to slow down your thoughts and make a good decision about what you are about to do.

I also talk about the consequential thinking method, or "thinking ahead." The ability to apply consequential thinking allows people to assess their choices, anticipate how people will react and follow their intentions. Consequential thinking is about imagining the upsides and downsides of our actions. *Thinking* about what you are doing, and if it is the safe, that correct choice can help give you that edge as an athlete. It may also help save your life.

For all of the time I spent telling Jordan to make good decisions, I didn't necessarily teach him the critical thinking skills he needed in order to make those decisions for himself. It was one thing to tell my son about my own bad decisions, but something entirely different to give him the tools he needed to think critically about these decisions before he made them.

Most, if not all, student athletes have or have had dreams to play at the professional level of competition one day. Keep in mind that only 1.6 % of college football players actually make it to the NFL. I always used to tell Jordan the idea of him playing at the next level was realistic.

Quite a few of his teammates were either being drafted or walking on to some NFL teams. We'd discuss the time frame and income he'd possibly make. I always told him the average time most players play in the NFL is only 3.1 years. If he did make it, he would be retired before the age of 28. He'd have to get his degree and most definitely save his money.

 I wanted him to have a realistic view of an average career in the NFL, I wanted him to look at the big picture of what playing professionally meant, so he could make sure he got a degree, saved his money and had a backup plan. I wanted to make sure he was prepared for what professional sports would be like. However, there were so many other things that I needed to teach my son to make sure he was mentally and physically prepared to play at the next level.

Any student athlete that wants to play at the college level and on to a professional level of competition, should ask themselves if they are willing to do the following things:

- Master the mundane of the boring fundamentals until they become second nature.
- Always take care of their mental health.
- Always take care of their physical health.
- Listen to their body.
- Do not indulge in drinking alcohol or taking illegal substances no matter what their friends are doing.
- Use the W.A.I.T. method.
- Become a consequential thinker.

-       Be prepared to eat, sleep and breathe your sport at least 16 hours a day.

These are the types of habits that will not only make students better athletes and safer players, but ones that will help them in their journey to reach the next level and stay at the next level once they get there.

Helping Parents to Parent Smarter

That old adage about "parents parenting and coaches coaching" will likely continue to permeate throughout youth sports. However, this doesn't mean that parents can't be smarter about their role in their child's athletics, and that they can't be more involved with the coaches—more specifically what questions they ask these coaches.

As I've mentioned before, I never thought to ask coaches any safety questions during Jordan's recruitment process. Like many parents who aren't in the medical field, we assumed they would know. As part of our outreach with The Jordan McNair Foundation, I don't just speak to kids, I speak to parents and coaches as well. It is so important for parents to be involved with the health and safety of their children while they're playing sports.

I always give parents a list of questions they should ask coaches at any level of sports activity their child is involved in. These go beyond the famous two: "How much playing time will my child get?" And, "Why is my child not getting more playing time?" They should include questions like this:

"Coach, what emergency action plan does your program have in place in the event that my child gets injured?"

"Who will call me in the event my child gets injured?"

"Where is the closest hospital?"

"Who will ride in the ambulance with my child if I'm not at the game or practice?"

"Where is the closest fire station?"

"Where is the closest police station?"

"Do you have athletic trainers at practices and games?"

"If my child has an allergic reaction to an insect bite or has an asthma attack is someone prepared to act? Will you be able to administer his or her Epi pen or asthma pump?"

"Will there be a cold-water tub at every practice or game especially during spring and summer months?"

"Will there be an AED machine available or close by?"

"Coach, what training has your staff regarding an emergency action plan, and do they have recent training certificates to prove this?"

Parents, these should be on your list of questions beyond your inquiries on playing time. These questions should be asked and answered to your level of comfort before you let your child play at any level of competition. Your coach, whether for Pee-Wee t-ball or college football, should be able to answer these questions. If these questions aren't answered, then you might seriously consider your student athlete playing for another program that can comfortably answer the questions you have.

As parents, we need to have more conversation around this subject. However, we need to know just as much safety information as the people we're entrusting our student athletes lives to.

It's a tough feeling for the parents who've lost a child to a sports injury to hear the coach give a philosophical reason on why your child died, especially when it is the same coach that they trusted to do the right thing. Tonya and I did not ask these questions. We did not think we would need to. But I'm begging you now, always ask these questions, *please*. They can make all of the difference in the world.

Educating Coaches to Coach Safer

The role of a coach extends beyond just teaching an athlete *how* to play a sport. Coaches assist athletes in developing to their full potential. They are responsible for training athletes by analyzing their performances, instructing in relevant skills and by working with them to mentally understand the game. There are so many youth coaches out there that donate their time to helping develop our young student athletes and to build these communities at the youth level.

Coaches also hold a lot of power and influence over our young people. Young "coachable" players are taught to follow their instructions, listen to their advice and work hard to make their coaches happy. I have seen what happens when this sense of power gets out of control. I have also seen what happens when coaches are better educated on how to make sure their kids are safe when they're participating.

Within the first year of The Jordan McNair Foundation, we trained over 3,500 people on the signs, symptoms and prevention of heat-related injuries. When training coaches, it is a different conversation from the ones you have with parents and student athletes. The most consistent fear from all coaches is that a student athlete will hurt, or worse, on their watch.

In addition to educating coaches on what they can do, we also encourage youth coaches to start paying for athletic trainers to come to their games.

Most programs at the AAU and the high school level don't have the budget to have an athletic trainer, however, they are significant to the health and safety of our student athletes.

Coaches at the youth and AAU levels typically get donations from parents to pay for a referee to officiate their games. I encourage coaches to take up a collection for an athletic trainer as well. Our foundation has used an organization called Go 4 Ellis that helps pair youth programs with per diem athletic trainers—and I believe that every coach should be taking advantage of resources like this.

I know that Jordan's story opened the eyes of a lot of sports programs across America. Coaches are regular people too. Ones that have a passion to help mold and the develop our young people. They volunteer their time, work with or commit themselves to help us as parents through the social nutrition of sports. But they can also make mistakes.

There have been over 60 heat-related deaths at the AAU, high school and collegiate level. I don't think any of these coaches maliciously said, "I'm going to kill a child today," when they showed up that morning. However, they clearly weren't educated on prevention and safety measures that should have been in place when the injury or fatality happened on their watch. Awareness, education and prevention of heat-related injuries empower us all to keep our young people and student athletes safe.

I have had many so many coaches come up to us after a health and wellness trainings and say they have been coaching for 20-30 years and I didn't know any of this information. My response is always the same "Coach, you and your staff now know how to keep those kids safe."

Youth sports has been around and will hopefully be around for a long time. The more that parents, coaches and students work together to keep it safe, the longer future generations can keep enjoying all of the benefits that sports have to offer. We just need to keep working, keep educating and keep empowering those involved, until we can rest assured that no sports culture can ever be labeled as "toxic" again.

April 30, 2020

As I've been sitting down to write this book, I've come to the realization the that this is my first real opportunity to grieve the loss of Jordan. I had no idea that my tears would flow the way that they have since taking on this project. The memories and emotions I've had to revisit have been therapeutic.

Every article I've had to reference for a date, or an exact piece of information has been challenging to read. Watching every video interview that Tonya and I gave at the height of our pain of losing Jordan was as heart-wrenching as it was motivating. The questions my editor asked me to answer regarding my feelings and emotions at the time of every chapter made me feel anger, frustration and elation when I thought through every part of this story.

Every text message I reread between Jordan and I before he got injured made my day. I have a picture of Jordan and I at Universal Studios in Orlando on my desk. That is where we went for his 18th birthday in March of 2017. Who knew that'd be our last trip together? I look at that picture and talk to him every day. I ask him to give me his input or send me a sign when I have difficulty writing, because some memories took me places that I've been trying to evade in my mind. I also look at that same picture and apologize just as many times for not protecting him or preparing him with information I just didn't have knowledge of at the time.

The laughter, the tears and the motivation to complete this project has been beyond rewarding and therapeutic for me. I didn't write this on my own, Tonya's memories of certain events, when my own fell short, were essential to making sure I got every detail right. Jordan has been smiling down on me with every word typed and every idea that came to my mind.

Jordan's influence on me started March 3, 1999 at 4:17 in the morning when he came into this world. For 19 years, I always thought my actions and my efforts to be a good example as a father and human being was teaching him something. Little did I know, he was actually preparing me those 19 years to reveal the artist that I'm becoming.

Writing this book has been like painting a picture of Jordan's life. It has taken so much careful thought and decisiveness to put the colors in the right places of the canvas, so you can see this story as whole. Not just the parts you read online, but the whole story. I used each color to highlight another part of our story, to pull your attention in another direction. I have never created something like this before, I have never had the time or patience to.

I just thought art was never my thing, until I've looked back on this book and realized the real masterpiece isn't the story itself, it's my son, Jordan Martin McNair.

I've written most of this book during the COVID-19 pandemic. The virus has slowed us all down, allowing us to look at what really matters in life. It's amazing what we can pull out of ourselves when we're forced to do so. I started working on this book last October. I'd pick it up and put it down whenever I had time. Who knew our lives would be so interrupted by this pandemic to make us see what's really important in life? Our faith, our families and ourselves.

All of this uncertainty in our world only solidifies what I've believed this entire time—that the universe makes no mistakes, and everything happens when the time is right. There is always a greater purpose, even in life's most difficult obstacles. I learned this when I went to jail and found sobriety. I learned it when I lost Jordan and found a new purpose to help others. And I'm learning it now, as I take the time to slow down amidst the chaos in our world and grieve my son.

I always thought Jordan's greater purpose in life was football, but his purpose turned out to be much greater than playing on Sundays. His purpose was to help save young people, like him, who love sports, because sports are fun. I spent all of Jordan's life telling him to be a better version of me, and he was. And now, as I continue to promote his legacy and spread his mission, I only hope I can become a version of him.

That I can work hard, be kind and always have a big, wider-than-my-face smile on as I honor my son with each and every person I meet.

The Jordan McNair Foundation would like to recognize the following student athletes who lost their lives to heat-related injuries.

Marquese Meadow, Morgan State University 2014

Zach Martin Polsenberg, Riverdale High School 2017

Braeden Bradforth, Garden City Community College 2018

Imani Bell, Elite Scholars Academy 2019

Hezakiah Walters, Middleton High School 2019

Preston Birdsong, Tennessee Tech 2010

Rashidi Wheeler, Northwestern 2001

Erick Plancher, University of Central Florida 2001

Chad Wiley, North Carolina A&T 2008

Michael King, University of Indianapolis 2000

Eraste Autin, University of Florida 2001

Doug Schmeid, Illinois Wesleyan University 2005

Vince Bernardo, Shippensburg University 2006

Sam Collins, Huntingdon College 2008

Tyler Heintz, Kent State University 2017

*Please note, this is not a complete list of athletes. With some nontraumatic exertion-related fatalities, the cause of death is open to interpretation.

Afterword

As I was writing *Can My Child Play?* my thoughts consistently were filled with this list of student athletes that passed away from complications of heat-related injuries. There are more than 30 total who have passed at the youth and collegiate levels of competition.

I could not stop thinking that there was a cycle of poor decision making from coaches in the world of youth sports. And that these bad decisions were still being made. As I investigated these names, I began to see that this wasn't just a football injury but a student athlete injury. It can take the lives of young people, no matter what sport they play.

In 2019, we didn't lose any student athletes at the collegiate level of competition from a heat-related injury. This is the first time this has happened in 21 years. I do believe that Jordan's death opened a lot of eyes at the college level. I saw a lot of schools who didn't want that stigma of what happened at Maryland to happen to them. I noticed that more schools in the NCAA made the appropriate changes to ensure the safety of their student athletes. I am sure that those that may have taken a heat-related injury lightly before, have changed their thought process moving forward.

This is a positive step forward, but it is not enough.

I wish I could say that youth and high school sports are making similar transformations.

In 2019, we lost a female cheerleader, a female basketball player and a few teenage football players. All of them were at practice. All were running some type of conditioning drill.

These are situations where having a cold-water tub nearby could have saved their lives.

All of these families have unwillingly become members of a club none of us want to be members of. I, along with Laurie Diagorno, from The Zach Martin Foundation have discussed the idea of reaching out to all the families to make some type of connection. To bring us all together. I know that the grief of losing a child looks different for everyone and that the processing of that grief can take people in different directions.

Our lives will never be the same. I'm sure you all, like Tonya and I, questioned God and questions yourselves a great deal. I'm sure you ask, "why my child?" more times than you can count. I wanted to acknowledge that you are thought of, every day. I know how difficult it is, and my prayers will always be with you and your families.

I'm often asked how Tonya and I do it. How we handled losing a child and jumping into advocacy immediately.

We have a strong faith in a higher power. We also have love for ourselves, one another, and every parent of a student athlete out there.

There have been small things that have helped me along the way. In fact, at Jordan's funeral, I met an older family member for the first time in my life. She gave me a handwritten note that stated:

"Children aren't ours; they're gifts from God. One day we'll have to return that gift. Hopefully later than sooner, but we will have to return that gift we've been blessed with one day. Enjoy, love and do everything you can with your gift while you have it in your possession."

Tonya and I had no regrets on what we did with our gift Jordan. We chose not to beat ourselves up for what we didn't teach him up until that point in his 19 years. We taught him everything we both knew. How could we beat ourselves up about what we didn't know? We refused to let grief negatively consume us and lead us into a rabbit hole of depression and despair. Our grief went into making a difference and turning our pain into a purpose of educating as many as we could with our story.

One of the first UMD alumni I spoke to after Jordan's passing was a student athlete who played on the football team in the 1950s. He spoke of Charles "Sonny "Lohr who passed in 1959 from complications of a heat-related injury he suffered on the football field during conditioning drills. I wanted to acknowledge a fellow Maryland Terrapin teammate who I'm sure was remembered by his teammates and his family. It saddens me to see that 60 years after Sonny's death, tragedies like this were still happening at the University of Maryland.

I wanted to include that list of the student athletes, in addition to Jordan, who have passed from heat-related injuries since the year 2000 because I believe it is an important list for the world to see. I'm sure I missed some of the names, and I'm sure there will be additional names added to this list. I can only hope that one day the list stops growing.

All of these student athletes as well as their families should be acknowledged and remembered in this advocacy of keeping our children safe. I send my most sincere acknowledgements to the athletes and their families I didn't put on this list as well.

Our continued thoughts are with you. I hope that this small gesture gives you a sense of peace, knowing we are advocating on behalf of your student athlete's sacrifice. And I promise you, we won't stop working in their honor to make a difference and to save the lives of as many young people as we can.

Marty McNair

Acknowledgements

I would like to thank Tonya Wilson for being so impactful in my life. Without her, I wouldn't have had my beautiful gift of a son, Jordan. Her memories of our story got me through at times when I was trying to paint a picture of our experiences. Thanks to my mother, Susie McNair, for loving me unconditionally. My father, Doug McNair, my biggest critic, thank you for encouraging me to write this in my own words, even during our heated discussions of how something should be written.

Thank you to our village, for every family member who invested their personal piece of love into me and Jordan. This includes Nana "Lenora Wilson," our family's matriarch, Aunt Shan, Uncle Jermaine, Uncle Lonnie, Aunt Stacia, Grandfather Richard and his wife Jeannette, DJ, Deairra, Oshea, the triplets, Joseph, Jayden, Jayla and Tonya's fiancé, House.

Thank you to all the village members I didn't name, your support is always appreciated. Much love and gratitude to Cousin Ojeda who was the spiritual nucleus that kept me and the rest of our immediate family together those two weeks Jordan was fighting for his life in the hospital. Her valuable nonprofit insight has continually given us the foresight to build and develop The Jordan McNair Foundation.

Many thanks to our legal team at Murphy, Faulcon and Murphy for the genuine love, support, motivation, and guidance to look at the big picture of using our national voice to make a difference. Many thanks to Zach McDaniels, the team's strategic advisor who got us in the right doors at the right times every time. Thank you, Zach, for listening to many of my ideas with this project. Thanks to my good friends Mike and Kia Locksley for all of the support on the days we've needed it the most.

Thanks to our other sons, Ellis McKennie III, Kareem Montgomery and the brave young men who stepped up and did the right thing. Thanks to my good friend and workout buddy Matt Fazzino for his contribution to this project.

Most importantly, my appreciation goes my business partner, Carlton Carrington, who ran the business while allowing me to complete this project. All love, Ace.

Applause to my editor Lisa M. for digging and prodding at me, and taking me a few places I didn't want to go while painting the pictures of my emotional and mental thoughts while writing this. Lisa, you're right, we have a book here. Thank you.

My love, respect, admiration and appreciation go to my wife Dawn for reading my chapter drafts over and over again, listening to my ideas constantly and just being there unconditionally.

For more information on The Jordan McNair Foundation, please visit us at:

TheJordanMcNairFoundation.org

We also encourage you to visit some of our trusted partner organizations to learn more about heat-related injuries:

The Gavin Class Foundation
Yoltfoundation.org

The Zach Martin Foundation
ZachMartinFoundation.com

Zach Polsenberg's Heat Severity Charity
PolsenbergCharity.org

TeamSafe Sports
TeamSafeSports.com

If you need to hire an athletic trainer for your child's youth sports activities, please visit:
Go4ellis.com

Made in the USA
Middletown, DE
01 July 2020